THE SIDE HUSTLE SOLUTION

FREDERIKE HARMS

AND CO.

DEDICATION

For Harriet
May you never hold back from going after your dreams.

CONTENTS

INTRODUCTION

There I was, wedged between two slightly overweight gentlemen sweating in their suits, on the 6:58 am train from Farnham to London Waterloo. Once I got there, I still had to cram myself onto the Waterloo & City Line for one stop - an experience to be avoided if you're even the slightest bit agoraphobic (which I am).

Bearing this daily commute in mind, I'm sure you understand how the excitement and happiness I had felt when I secured the first contract for MY business had worn off rapidly. But let me tell you how I ended up on trains and the underground on a daily basis, against my better judgement.

It was a 9 am on a Monday morning when I looked at my boss and said: "I want to discuss my exit plan." And with that, I resigned from a well-paid job with nothing lined up and what felt like 3987 bills to pay each month.

Good effort for someone that suffers from an anxiety disorder...

I left that meeting relieved, but terrified. All. At. Once. Quite the mix of emotions. I was interrupting punching the air with a facepalm, wondering what was going to come next.

It had only been a few weeks since I was in bed on a Tuesday afternoon, paralysed with worry over not being able to keep my job and therefore pay my bills because of my anxiety. I felt worse and worse, and it turned into a vicious cycle of anxiety, stress, worry, physical symptoms, sad thoughts, more anxiety, more stress, more worry, more physical symptoms and so many more sad thoughts.

How bad does it have to get for me to get the message?

This is the question I always come back to. How unappreciated, how unhappy, how physically sick do I have to feel to take action and a step towards a better life?

In more cases than not, the anxiety and restlessness you feel is a message: the universe wants us to live our truth, knowing we can do better if only we'd believe in ourselves more and looked after ourselves better. The situations we feel most uncomfortable in are our most significant opportunities to grow. A change in that area of your life will have the greatest impact.

So, I got to that point where I knew I had to do something.

For me.

So, I did.

Deep down, I had faith that I have so much to offer and that I can get over anything that I'm scared of to live my best possible life. The world is my oyster, the sky is the limit.

And yes, I had a lot of the "Oh wow, I usually find a new job before quitting the one I have!", to which I had to reply with a sarcastic "Oh geez, really? I hadn't thought of that!" and move on.

I won't lie - I spent at least two nights crying, I didn't sleep much, but by the end of the week I was in a much better place and was actually excited for what was to come. I was fully aware that it's not always going to be easy and all sunshine and butterflies, but I also knew (and still know) that easy is not always better.

Because I had bills to pay and no significant savings, I quickly had to come up with a plan. I knew I wanted to do my own thing - this had always been my plan, and this seemed like a good opportunity.

I had ideas en masse, but I had to find something that (1) I'd get paid for quickly and that (2) would allow me to retain my lifestyle. So, I went with what most of us do and started a consultancy business doing exactly what I'd done in my corporate career: Project and Change Management.

It was the safe option: I knew exactly what I was doing, who'd need me and my services and I could get all the recommendations and testimonials I needed. I was confident and I had contacts, which meant I was able to secure my first contract within five days of quitting the job.

Phew.

I felt a massive relief, of course, and excitement. I was out there securing clients, making money for ME! And just like that, I registered a limited company, decided on a company name, enlisted a branding designer and found a website developer. I came up with a strategy and had calls with a number of my "ideal clients" to better understand their pain points. And before I knew it, public transport was my second home and I was desperately clinging on to the idea that I had made it!

I managed for a year, before it all came to a head as I was shovelling truly Italian Tiramisu into my mouth. All four of my new friends were looking at me expectantly with one or two encouraging nods thrown in. "Alright, you're right. I'm in the wrong business."

It was a special weekend that I spent in Firenze (Florence, for those of you that have never been) eating prosciutto e funghi pizza and handmade ravioli with sun-kissed basil and buffalo mozzarella, drinking prosecco and copious amounts of espresso, as well as catching melting gelato with my tongue in a way that cannot be described as sexy under any circumstances.

Oh, and I attended a two-day writing workshop with an amazingly talented copywriter I'd been following for years.

I set out to do this to get better at writing copy for my business. And then I had a meltdown. Partially due to the sweat-inducing and chaff-promoting heat, and partly because I froze every time someone asked me "So, what was it you do?"

I could not put it into words. My elevator pitch became more silent elevator than pitch. This was worrying.

Then, when we had to write down 10 birthday wishes that our ideal client would have I could not think of one. Like one that someone would whisper as they blow out the candles on their birthday cake, not one that you would find in an off-putting email written by that new - supposedly - up-and-coming coach that crafted their copywriting skill by reading "Sales for Dummies": "Always been wanting to step in your personal power?"

It was the final nail in the coffin. What was I doing if thinking about my ideal client didn't get me excited?

Of course, those tiny, little moments are life-changing and we know it. Deep down.

You just have to be brave enough to listen and not try and freeze out the knowledge with more gelato (yes, I am qualified to advise on this).

It was time to be brave and change paths. Again. I was equally excited and mortified.

I left Italy with a head buzzing with things I needed to do and new dreams. Not too long ago, this would have overwhelmed, frustrated and scared me, but now I knew what I had to do:

I needed to take action. Put one foot in front of the other.

My motivation for writing this book, and sharing some of my story and a whole load of actionable advice with you, is so that you can do the same.

Because success is down to mindset and action. I'll be covering both in the chapters of this book. I always tell my clients, if you take action, but don't really believe it'll make a difference, then it won't. Equally, if you believe, visualise and manifest like a champion, but don't take any action, then that doesn't work either.

It's the combination of both that makes the difference. I transformed my business after I started feeling passionate and excited about what I was doing and took consistent action to create my new - and desired - reality. This is your guide to doing the same.

A quick word on Side Hustles

Side hustles, or the concept of a part-time business, can take several shapes and forms. It could be that you're still employed by a company, full-time or part-time, while also building your business. Or you may be staying at home, raising your children and running a household, which is a full-time job (and then some) in itself as I'm sure we can all agree. You may be self-employed, but working a big corporate contract (like I am) while building your legacy. Or you may have a business, but decide you want to add an additional income stream that is separate from your existing operation. Lastly, you may be in a position, like many of my clients who have a successful business but want to change direction and pivot. They can't afford to just cut-and-run, so instead have to keep their existing business going to pay the bills while building up something new.

Whatever your situation is, a lot of the principles and actions that I'm describing in this book still apply. In fact, most of it can be applied to simply building a business - just that you could complete the work more quickly and launch!

Throughout the book, I often refer to a 9 - 5 or your corporate job for simplicity, but please know that this can be replaced with looking after kids, working a contract or running another business.

How to read this book

The book has a certain order which follows the tried-and-tested process and framework I use when I work with my clients on a 1:1 basis, so I can recommend you read it from front to back. The process steps are broken down into chapters, so it'll be easy for you to revisit some the information after you finished the book and are implementing what you've learned.

I have included a number of actions you can take and exercises you can complete to help you move forward with your business idea, so make sure you have a highlighter and notepad ready!

You can download any bonus resources from thesidehustlesolution.com where you'll also be able to leave me a message or ask a question.

For now, thank you for letting me walk beside you for part of this exciting journey and know that I'll be waiting for you at your dream destination with a bottle of champagne.

1

VISION

This first section of the book is focused on your end goal. If working as a Project Manager for over 15 years has taught me anything, it's that you need to know where you going in order to ever actually get there. This is possibly also the biggest difference between me and other business coaches, and that applies whether you're building a side hustle or a full-time business: I want you to design a life of freedom with structure and purpose - your business is the vehicle that enables that life.

In this first section, we're looking at that big dream of yours and turning it into something specific, so that you can use it as a guidepost when creating your business model. But before we do that, we need to address the biggest stumbling block on the entrepreneurial journey: your mindset. When it comes to limiting beliefs and excuses, I've heard them all and have used them all. Been there, done that, bought the t-shirt.

At the end of this first section, I want you to know what it is you want to make happen and I want you to believe that you can do it too.

Ready?

Buckle up - it's a wild, but exciting ride.

THE IMPORTANCE OF MINDSET

If cauliflower can be pizza, imagine what you can be!

I'm an action taker. Always have been. Forever having several projects on the go. I've been self-employed one way or another ever since I left school - even during those times when I was also employed, I would support businesses on a freelance basis or work on my own ideas in my spare time.

I'd pride myself on the fact that I could get more done than anyone else I knew. There'd never be any unread emails in my inbox nor little red dots with the number of unread notifications on my mobile phone screen. I'd say 'yes' to anyone that'd ask for my help; putting out fires all over the place. And man, I loved it.

People needed me. ME! I felt needed and I could add things to my to do list, which I could then tick off - one of my favourite things in the world. Getting sh*t done.

Little did I know at the time that this whole approach covered up a major issue: I needed other people to give me validation. I didn't truly believe that I was worthy, that I could do it, that I had what it takes; unless someone else needed ME to help them out. Of course, people were coming to me over and over again, because I'd always say yes - just to get an ego boost. It was a win-win: They solved whatever problem they were confronted with (well, I solved it for them) and I got my daily dose of validation.

It was also ridiculous. I was constantly busy, but so bored. Admittedly, the projects I managed were getting bigger and bigger. More and more eyes were on them, which can be a great opportunity, BUT there were two problems: (1) I never got any feedback or recognition, because when you do your job well you rarely hear about it; and (2) I still didn't understand that the bigger projects and the increased responsibilities were down to my hard work and skill.

When I applied the above approach to my own business - always taking action, always saying yes to all the opportunities - it backfired. All of a sudden, I was terribly busy doing work that either didn't pay well or at all (which

I did to build valuable relationships and/or get testimonials) or emotionally took me straight back to my corporate days of boredom - and now I didn't even get health insurance and a mediocre annual bonus in exchange anymore.

It took me another couple of years to figure out the missing variable: my mindset!

I now know that success is a result of action AND mindset. You can be busy day in, day out BUT if you don't think you can achieve what you dream of, then the action you take won't be directed and productive (see my story above for reference).

The same applies to the opposite, of course. We can be the greatest at visualising our success as we surround ourselves with vision boards and other inspiration, BUT you'll never build that 7-figure business and buy that 5-bedroom house with the double garage and a huge open plan kitchen, dining room and lounge unless you consistently take action that takes you closer to the dream outcome.

Mindset + Action = Success

This was a huge stumbling block for me as I started building my business. I absolutely had the big dreams: I want to be able to work from anywhere, with clients from all corners of the world. I want to go out to eat ice cream with my niece and nephew in Germany, meet my friends for brunch at Nomo in Soho and have lunch meetings at Manhatta - a restaurant on the 60th floor of an office building in downtown, New York. I want to attend workshops in Florence and write my newsletters from a poolside sun bed in Dubai.

I want to be able to meet my clients in nice hotels, not beige meeting rooms with questionable stains on the brown carpet. I want to be in a room with people that are as passionate as I am, but also know the same struggles and will jump on a call with me when I need someone to tell me that it's going to be ok.

And when I'm not doing that, then I want to be able to take days off to spend with my baby girl whenever I please, cuddle my dog between calls, have time to go for a walk when a headache sets in and have dinner with my love. I want to be able to take the afternoon off because the sun is shining and rain is forecast for tomorrow. I want to be able to FaceTime with my 5-year-old nephew at 11:30 am when he needs to show me his new tricks as a fire artist and then be able to call my brother to let him know that his son has candles and lighters in his room...

So, all that was missing for me was belief. The belief that I could have all of those things. That I was, in fact, meant for more.

You're meant for more

Turns out, I wasn't the only one that struggled with this. So, before we dive in, I want to address possibly the biggest limiting belief I come across constantly when working with my clients, so that we can get this out of the way and clarify from the start that you are indeed ready and meant to turn your dreams into reality.

I had a real good think about what made you and me different from those that didn't wake up every morning wishing for their own empire.

Why me? Who am I to do this?

Well, there are the five signs that tell you that you're meant for something bigger:

1. You have big dreams
Your mind was made up ever since meeting Carrie, Samantha, Charlotte and Miranda in 1998: you want to live in New York City. Your dream car is a Porsche Cayenne and you are pretty damn sure you will own a holiday home in Italy by 2023, paid for in cash. You allow yourself the kind of dream that makes most people roll their eyes and you're sure that you'll achieve it. You are following people on Instagram that have achieved it, so you know you can too. Of course, you have moments of

doubt - who doesn't – but ultimately, your dream is bigger than that, which is why you're holding this book in your hands right now.

2. You constantly feel restless

It's uncomfortable - like that hen party for your work colleague where you hardly know anyone. You agreed to attend, but you really can't wait for it to be over so you can be back on your sofa in your Lululemon pants with a cup of coffee. Experiences that don't contribute to your development or allow you to recharge your batteries make you tense. This can be boring tasks at work, the facial you booked during the spa day that gives you too much time to think but not enough space to do or the after work drinks with the team following a successful project go live. You know it's gotta be done, but your mind is already five steps ahead.

3. You get frustrated with negativity

Being on the phone with your friend who hates her boss but won't apply for other jobs drains you. Your dodging calls from your sister who moved to what feels like the end of the world for "the love of her life" but hates it there, after she ignores every single suggestion you make for her to meet people. You know life is not perfect and it's not realistic for everyone to be happy 100% of the time, however, you don't understand or have time for people that don't help themselves. You work hard to be positive and optimistic and deep down know you don't want to allow energy-draining people in your life anymore, even if that admission scares you.

4. You take action

While other people set up a direct debit for their weekly lottery ticket and talk about all the things they will buy when they win, you have done the maths and know your chances of becoming a multi-millionaire are much higher if you just work for it - which is what you do. You think about all the ways that you could make your dreams come true and try and come up with strategies - for example, you know that working as a florist for someone else will never get you that racehorse that it top of your list of extravagant-new-millionaire purchases. Yes, it's scary and overwhelming and you don't have it all figured out, but you know that it will take more than spending £2.50 on a piece of paper.

5. You have all the ideas

You know that you can't expect a different outcome if you keep doing the same thing. So, you don't. You love coming up with solutions to other people's problems and while you know that it is sometimes a lot more difficult to do on your own when you are stuck in a particular situation, you are aware of the challenge and get help. You are solution-focused and inventive. Even creative - never-mind the fact that you can't draw and therefore think you aren't. When you have different ideas and solutions, you don't procrastinate, but go for it. Trial and error is a thing. Sometimes it doesn't go as planned or doesn't bring the result you were looking for, but you don't generally regret anything. Everything happens for a reason!

Do you recognise yourself in the list above? Be honest! I thought so. Time's up on your excuses - from here on out you're the entrepreneur you've always wanted to be, hustling hard to build that life you're dreaming of.

Understanding your excuses and limiting beliefs

"What if that author would've never written your favourite book because there are so many books out there already?"

"Yes! And what if your favourite Italian restaurant had never opened because the owner thought that there were loads of great Italian restaurants and no one needed another one?"

"Ooooooooor what if Prada had never designed handbags because no one needs an expensive handbag when they can use a plastic bag?"

Ok, I made the last one up, but imagine that! What a nightmare!

The first two questions are real. Two of my girlfriends

asked me this after I had just told them that - SURELY - no one needed another coach in the world. This was my favourite excuse and my biggest resistance on the path to building my dream business.

They made their point and they made it well. I didn't have a comeback and didn't want to imagine a world without my favourite pizza place - I don't have time for that sort of negativity.

"Fine, you're right."

And that was that. Decision made.

We are always quick to come up with excuses and lots of them - many of which will also sound familiar to you. You just have to admit it to yourself before you can take action to overcome them. There's a whole variety of excuses that we use to hold ourselves back from making our dreams a reality, but there are a few that seem to come up again and again. I want to share a list of those with you and also tell you why it's an excuse and not a valid reason not to do something.

Time

There aren't enough hours in the day. Ever. I know that. You know that. Everyone knows that. Still, some people seem to manage to learn Italian or build up a business when they get home from work. As the saying goes: If you want it bad enough, you'll find the time. If not, then you'll find an excuse.

We'll go into more detail of how to free up time to work on your business when your days are already filled to the brim. But while at first glance it may feel like a practical problem, it's also a mindset shift. Next time you're trying to say that you don't have time for something, say "That's not important enough to me right now" instead and see how that feels. For some things it may feel uncomfortable, but you'll also (possibly secretly) think that it's true. However, if it bothers you more than it should, then challenge yourself on it. See if it possibly is more important than something else, and that it's actually something else that's holding you back - such as fear of failure. Time is finite. There are 24 hours in each day, which means you have to give up one thing to be able to have time for something else. At least in the short-term. It's up to you to decide if the short-term pain is worth the long-term gain.

Circumstances

It's difficult because of the wedding next year. Or you have a new boss, so you need to be focused on the job. Or your daughter is just starting school. Or your husband has moved roles. Or your pet rabbit has diarrhoea. I get it. My rabbit used to constantly struggle. The thing is though, I have spent most of life waiting for the perfect time; for something to happen so it'd be easier; for "things to quieten down a bit" so I could focus. Let me tell you: It ain't gonna happen. It's now or never.

Can you think of a time when your life was perfect and would have stayed like that long enough for you to build a whole business? Businesses aren't built overnight, so even if one thing falls into place, something else will come up that will need your attention. This is exactly one of the reasons why I wanted to build a business: so I was in control and could decide what to focus my time and attention on. You probably had thoughts along the lines of the following running through your head in early 2020 as you were rearranging your 3-bedroom mid-terraced house to somehow fit in two offices and three school desks: How on earth am I going to work full-time, homeschool my children and not lose my mind while I'm only allowed out of the house once a day? It was a trigger for many to really look at their life and take back control. Building a business the right way means that, yes, you'll work the odd weekend to get something new and exciting out there, but it also means you can make the decision to scale back when a pandemic hits the world out of nowhere. That's the aim, right?

Knowledge

Let me guess... You need to get a degree or and at

least another 4 courses to be qualified enough. It would also be great to have a few more years of experience before you go for it (whatever "it" is). I'm the same: I have two degrees, several qualifications and I am a recovering online course junkie. I actually use only very few of the things covered by those courses in my business or life.

After spending over 15 years as a Project Manager, running global change programmes, there's one thing I know for sure: You can't know everything. And no one expects you to. It's actually much more important to know what you don't know and to own that. No one will force you to sell something you're not comfortable with. It's ok to tell a prospective client that you can't help them with something, but that you'd be more than happy to recommend someone else they could speak to.

And something Denise Duffield-Thomas said beautifully: You don't have to be the guru. You're a contributor. You share your view and your approach, based on your experience.

Money

Money is a lot like time. As in 'time is money', I guess. Duh. In our dream life, at least 95% of us have more time or more money or both. There always seems to be a lot of month left at the end of the money and it's difficult to decide what we could cut back on to have some spare to spend on that business coach or graphic designer for our side hustle. For many of us, having more money to do the things we want to do is one of the key reasons we're setting out on this journey.

Same as with time above, it's figuring out what is important enough and what can move the needle for you the most (when spending money on outside help). You will find it - even if it means you have to give up paying for that gym membership you never use - or you will figure out how to DIY it. Where there is a will, there is a way.

Energy

"I'd love to, but I just don't have the energy right now." Have you heard this from someone or thought this yourself before?

To be honest, this is a big one for me: I have a special talent for not looking after myself very well when I get stressed. So when I'm tired, I eat a lot of ham and mushroom pizza, the odd portion of Chicken Nuggets and tiny tubs of Ben & Jerry's to keep me going, which is not exactly fuelling my body. And then I go from having little energy to having no energy. BUT I know that now. So I also know that this is not a reason not to do something, because I could sort myself out. It's down to me. Or YOU!

If you feel like you don't have the energy, then take steps to get to get to a better place. It's something you need to learn to do anyway. Building a business part-time or full-time is draining and it's hard to switch off when it's all down to you. So, if this is your excuse not to take your idea forward, then make 'Increasing Energy' one of your initial actions.

And guess what: It will give you so much more energy when you finally do what you want to do!

Age

No, you are not 10 years too young but three years too old. If there is something that you keep wishing for, hoping for, thinking about and dreaming of, then you are at the perfect age! If you need the evidence, then search online for examples of entrepreneurs that made a million before they turned 20 or entrepreneurs that started late in life. You'll find plenty of examples of both and it's time that you take steps to make it onto one of those lists if your age is something you're worrying about.

Failure

Of course you're afraid that things may not go the way you planned - we're all perfectionists at heart, especially when we are taking a leap out of our comfort zone. BUT as Catherine Cooke says: "If you're not making mistakes, then you're not making decisions." Mistakes and failures are lessons. Nothing more. Although it can feel uncomfortable and painful at the time, failure is actually a key method of learning, developing and re-evaluating. I know it's an old example, but you only learned to walk after falling on your cute, little, nappy-padded backside over and over and over again.

Sometimes a failure isn't even a failure at all. It can take years to really reflect on a situation and connect all the dots. More often than not, you'll find that the "failure" was never even a failure in the first place. You'll see the growth between then and now and be proud of what you have accomplished, and the different paths you have taken since that day. Also, failure strengthens our capacity to adapt. Having the power to get back up again after a fall shows resilience and determination; the ability to then shift your work or lifestyle to accommodate the change should not be underestimated. It's a trait that is crucial in an ever-changing world and will place you in a stronger position when situations do arise that steer you from your path.

Failure allows us to get better at recognising success. Periods of difficulty make the good times shine. How often do you stop and really pat yourself on the back for a win? I'll bet that you find it easier to lay out your shortcomings. I know I do. The beauty of failure is it allows the shade to bring out the light. We learn to appreciate and really celebrate success, because we can see how much better it makes us feel than the other stuff. You have to take the good with the bad. After all, there's no rainbow without the rain.

Failure also makes us more relatable. It's human: there are no two ways around it. Giving yourself permission to fail makes you more relatable as a business owner and a human being. Your audience will empathise with you, building on the "know, like and trust" factor. In turn, you will find yourself at the helm of stronger relationships: the core component of a successful, influential business.

Another advantage of 'failing' is that it gives you new ideas. Failure is part and parcel of new ideas. Acknowledging that something doesn't work the way we want it to forces us to re-evaluate the entire product of the process; why doesn't it work and what can we do to make it better? This could be a small shift, a new product or a gap in the market that you identify needs filling. Whatever it is, it is an opportunity.

If this wasn't a pep talk that made you (almost) look forward to failing, then I don't know what is!

It's already been done

It's the one I started with above: "But it's already been done? No one needs another one!" And yes, they do. Your voice, your views, your experience is unique to you. You are the only person in the world that can share your gift and message. In a lot of ways it is actually easier to go into an established market, because at least you know there is a demand for what you have to offer. I have recently spent some time working on my money mindset. I read one book which had a list of further suggested reading at the back, so I ordered at least half of those books right there and then. In total, I probably have now read at least 10 books on how to change your money mindset and I still have a further five or so on my bookshelf. Most of them have the same or a very similar message, but each author has added their personal view and their different ways of implementing the advice. Some resonated with me more than others, but generally it's been good to keep reading the advice over and over because we usually have to hear it more than once for it to sink in.

So, don't let this excuse hold you back. Instead look for what you can do differently to appeal to the customer *you* want to work with and how you can add your unique view and voice - something we'll look at in more detail as part of the process in this book.

Self-worth

My guess is that this is the true reason you're holding back and most of the other excuses in this list are actually just cover-ups because it's so hard to admit. I didn't believe in myself for a long time, and it's what bothers me the most when I speak to my friends: They are unhappy with their situation, but don't believe they will be able to make the change to live the life they deserve. They think they got lucky being in the job they are in. It's heartbreaking.

That idea of being lucky and not feeling like we are worth more is closely linked to impostor syndrome, something that almost everyone experiences at one time in their life. This feeling of not being good enough, worrying about being found out as a fraud, the idea that we got lucky or fooled someone to get to where we are. It's so easy to recognise in others, but so hard to admit to in ourselves. As I said, I was constantly feeling frustrated with my friends, who were settling for roles that they had outgrown and managers that didn't appreciate them the way they deserved, but I couldn't see that the same applied to me.

Instead, I was working extra hard and all the hours to make sure I was ahead of the game. Or I stood still and procrastinated, using all of the excuses (that list you've just been reading is my masterpiece) which totally made sense to me. Whenever something worked out and others would point this out, I'd shrug it off and tell them that "I didn't really do all that much" or that "I just did my job" while assuring them that "anyone could do it". I always waited for something else to happen and then things would get better. Or I would be better (= happy).

Until that one day when I had a breakthrough. In a Starbucks. With an extra shot, short, black Americano in hand. There were tears too, as I recognised how I had let my low sense of self-worth dictate how I showed up in the world. And with that, I set out on a journey to change my life that took several years, but was so worth it. My life is not perfect (hell, at the time of writing this, we've all been stuck at home for the best part of a year, so no one's is), but the choices I now make are about me, my happiness and those I love.

The thing with imposter syndrome or low self-worth is that it almost always stays with us throughout our life. We may work on and through it, just to move on to something new and with that push outside of our comfort zone and bang - there it is again. We feel out of our depth and as though we should know more than we do (we shouldn't!), which means we often give up or work extra, extra hard to make sure no one realises (which is unnecessary). And we're back in that spiral that we previously escaped after a lot of hard work and self-discovery.

There are whole (very good) books on this topic and it's not my area of expertise, but it is something I've struggled with all of my life and I know so many of my clients struggle with it too, so I needed to include it here. The first step always is recognition. Recognising our excuses for what they are, so that we can take steps to move past them. This is more true for low self-worth than any others. You're the only one that would ever know that this is the actual problem, so you need to own up to it. And as you do that, I want you to know that you're in very good company, because we've all been there and keep coming back for more.

To wrap this up, I want to say that it's ok not to be perfect. It's much more important that you take action consistently and that you see your excuses as challenges, not as the ultimate truth.

I have a policy for myself and those working with me and it's pretty straightforward:

NO EXCUSES.

Not now. Not ever. The word 'excuse' is officially scrapped from your vocabulary.

Nothing destroys a dream more than:

"I can't because…"

"I was going to but…"

"I wish I could, it's just…"

It's. Just. Nothing.

Do it. Do it now. After all, we only regret the opportunities we didn't take.

MAKING ROOM FOR GROWTH

"Success is not an accident, success is a choice."

STEPHEN CURRY

In the last chapter I introduced you to my success formula (mindset + action = success) and we spoke about how our mindset can hold us back from going after what we're meant for. Thankfully, taking action is not as much of a struggle for most of us (entrepreneurs are often activators) as mindset is, however, it can be that little bit more challenging when building your business part-time.

When starting a business, you need to be structured

and organised. In the corporate world, there are managers setting deadlines, colleagues demanding your input or work, and reporting cycles forcing you to deliver. When you start building something on your own, it's down to you to make it happen.

You have to strategise, plan and arrange your life to make it work. When it comes to side hustling, you have a lot less time to organise (YAY) which means you have a lot less… uuummm… time (BOOO). Not an excuse though, remember? We're fully committed to making it happen!

And whether you like to hear it or not - the number one cause of unfulfilled dreams is simple: lack of responsibility. It may sound harsh. It may sound blunt. But let's not beat around the bush.

You - and only you - can make your dreams happen.

Wishing and hoping (while it may feel exciting) won't cut it. To pull those dreams out of your head and into "real life" you need:

(a) a clear plan of action;

(b) an active role in making the *thing* happen; and

(c) the drive to push it forward.

Coincidentally, this is what I'm obsessed with and what this book is about. I believe that we all have the power within ourselves to achieve whatever we set our mind to. No ifs, ands or buts.

It won't always be easy. There'll be highs and there'll be lows, but, with clear and consistent steps (both physical and mental), you can take control and make it happen. This book is full of ideas on how.

The third section of this book is all about implementing the plans and the practical steps to building your business, but I want to quickly cover off some practical tips so you have time to read this book and create those plans, so that you're not failing before you're even getting started!

Freeing up time

The biggest challenge in building a side hustle is the many different directions you're being pulled into. So before you dive into actually mapping out the business and the steps to take to make it a reality, you need to think through how this is going to work practically.

For most of us it's bad enough with having a family that's always hungry when fish finger wraps with peas and a ton of mayonnaise isn't living up to the gluten-free expectations, a partner that wants to watch Star Wars with us (again…) and the friend that "can't believe we haven't seen each other in as long as it would take to grow a baby". Throw in a full-time job and you're nominated for superwoman of the year.

It's no surprise then that there aren't many of us that are crazy enough to also start our own business! We're tough as nails, and oh so proud of it.

The key to being able to juggle all these balls is productivity and effective time management. There are whole books on this and this isn't one of them, BUT I want to share some practical tips with you that have helped me be more productive.

Unnecessary meetings at your 9 - 5

These are my biggest pet hate, especially when it's a meeting to prepare a meeting. I mean, really? In at least 80% of cases, I'd rather go to the dentist than sit in the meeting, but it still seems to be everyone's favourite way to spend their workday.

And don't get me wrong: a meeting can absolutely be the best way to progress and resolve something quickly IF the right people are in the room and are prepared. Neither of which is usually the case. In fact, in a lot of cases, the people that are in the room are unsure why they are.

So this is what you can do if you're a participant (aka not in charge of the meeting):

- Whenever an invite comes through without a

note or agenda, I'll go back and ask what it is about to determine whether I am the right person to attend. Your time is precious, so don't just join something because the actual decision-maker isn't available. It won't speed up anything.

- Ask for information about what's to be discussed or an agenda (which should be a minimum anyway) so that you can prepare and add value.
- Be 100% present if you are attending, and be prepared. Don't dial into a conference call and then try to use that time to clear your inbox. Set an example. If you're there, be there. If you don't think it's valuable, then decline ahead of the meeting.

If you're organising a meeting:

- Make sure you identify the right decision-makers and find a time that they can all attend, so you don't have to have several meetings because you're going round in circles.
- Provide an agenda, so people know what it's about and can prepare.
- Capture minutes and distribute them as soon as possible after the meeting. Follow up to make

sure things get done - you won't need another meeting to 'check-in' if you have a good task management system that you can track progress on.

- Actively facilitate the conversation so you manage to speak about everything you need to cover off.

Always question the need for a meeting. Consider the time and therefore cost associated with a meeting: an hour's meeting may actually cost your company five hours productive time if five people attend. I know it'll feel like an uphill battle in most organisations, but if you don't try to change the world then who will, right? Even if you manage to get out of two meetings a week then that could be two extra hours of productive time.

By the way: I'm not suggesting that you use time during your workday to build your business (necessarily), but I want you to be as productive as possible so that you can spend the time outside of your day job on your side hustle. I know that many in the corporate space spend all day in meetings and then have to produce outputs in the evening - which, going forward, is your prime side hustle time and the time when you may be speaking to clients, etc.

Lack of organisation

Not being organised can have an impact in different ways. For one, it's a productivity blocker if you have time, but don't know what to work on next. So not having a plan and tasks broken down and prioritised will always slow you down. You'll spend 30 minutes looking through to-do lists and emails as well as doing some low-value activities such as responding to Facebook messages when you could have spent it brainstorming that new retreat you want to offer.

Another hurdle is if you know what you want to work on, but can't find the research or documents you need to complete the task. If your (virtual) office is all over the place and you have notes in apps, notebooks, diaries, Google docs, some documents in your filing cabinet, in-tray and scanned in the cloud, then good luck.

And I'm not telling you to only ever take notes in one place, because I love a pretty notebook with an inspirational quote on it (this person does not need an excuse to buy stationary....) but also use notes apps. However, I will tell you to take 15-30 minutes at the end of each week to organise your notes:

- capture actions in a task management system
- add notes and ideas to the relevant resource bank and

- schedule anything that's urgent or has a deadline.

This can be part of your weekly planning exercise or your weekly wrap up, as long as you make sure that it becomes part of a routine that you trust.

Side note: As long as we don't capture ideas/thoughts/scenarios/to-do's in a structured and explicit way, it will always be in the back of our mind and will pop into our thoughts and the most inconvenient times. Usually when we've just started working on a dreaded task and welcome any reason to do something else. You may have experienced this yourself when you remember to do something, but can't do it straight away. You forget, but it keeps popping into your head until you finally schedule a reminder in your phone app that will remind you that evening when you're home and you can finally stop thinking about it and focus on the task at hand. Decluttering your mind and writing things down is a small change with a huge impact - trust me.

Perfectionism

Also known as procrastination, this can cost us hours and days and months. We want to do the best job possible, which is understandable considering how much time, energy and money we spend on building our businesses.

However, this often means we don't take action at all. Or we take action, produce something great, but don't put it out there in the world where it could add value to our life or our customers lives. Accept that, by definition, half of your work will be below average, and do it anyway. The more you produce, the better you'll get at it and the better your output will be.

How does this cost us precious time? Remember that time you sat down to map out your business model and then remembered that you should really hoover the stairs because you saw some dog hair when you came up to your desk? And how your husband's sock drawer hasn't had the Marie Kondo treatment in at least two weeks and is ALL OVER THE PLACE, like there are blue socks mixed in with the black socks? Nightmare. And how you absolutely cannot build a business unless your desk looks like the one in the stock photo that your influencer of choice posted on Instagram? I know. Who can write a business plan without looking at a vase of blush pink peonies and matching copper coloured desk accessories! Well, turns out I can. And here's a hint: You can too!

Decisions

Decisions take time and headspace. In our house, it's all about what to have for dinner. If we don't meal plan and order the food shop to be delivered at the beginning of the week, it turns into a never ending discussion to take place every single day, followed by trips to the supermarket to pick up the spinach, grab some steaks or fresh coriander, because there's always at least one ingredient we haven't got in the house.

Removing as many decision points from your day as possible by either planning ahead, standardising processes, creating routines and checklists or even by practicing making quick decisions will make all the difference. A decision not yet made will always create noise in your mind and will be distracting.

There's another problem though, which really links to my point about perfectionism above: We want to avoid risks, so ideally make decisions once we feel we have all the information to run through every possible scenario and weigh up the options. But having all the information is not only near-impossible, but also only true for one moment in time. To quote Seth Godin: "Decisions are good even if the outcomes aren't." We can make the best decision possible without ever achieving the outcome we're dreaming of. The world around is changing too quickly for us to be able to forecast a definite outcome, but that doesn't mean we shouldn't make decisions and move forward. So don't wait for perfect because it'll never come. Don't think you need to complete another course or get another qualification, but start where you are with what you have.

Entrepreneurship is a process, not a destination, so nothing's set in stone.

When it comes to decisions, there are really only two options:

(a) you make the decision; or

(b) you figure out what information is missing for you to make an informed decision and you define an action to obtain that information, then make the decision.

By the way, 'sleeping on it' is fine, but it's only a valid excuse for one night.

Low levels of energy

Again, there are millions of books about this and many coaches and practitioners more qualified than me to advise on topics of well-being and health, but it's something I struggle with often and it's a very prevalent problem for those building side hustles, so I want to mention it here. I already mentioned this in my list of excuses and hinted at the fact that you need to get in control of this to be able to successfully run your business (it's a marathon, not a sprint - if you know what I mean).

Burnout is the known and obvious one, but it doesn't have to come to that for your body and mind to be productivity blockers and therefore time wasters. We think working ALL OF THE HOURS means we get more done, but we are oh-so-wrong.

Not getting enough sleep for a few nights, a cold, constant overwhelm and stress, not eating proper meals or not doing any exercise can all have an impact on your energy levels and therefore on your performance. It's hard to concentrate when tired or hungry, but both of those can be fixed quite easily.

Stress and overwhelm on the other hand will take a lot more effort to resolve. And counterintuitively, you'll have to take a break and a step back to be able to see the wood for the trees again. Again, awareness, transparency and having a plan are key when it comes to managing energy levels. There is nothing worse than remembering something crucial in the middle of the night or when you're in a focused session producing content, which you may as well write off as soon as you remember the 'other thing'.

Prepare as much as you can, so you can have time off to exercise, prepare nutritious meals, manage the important but boring tasks and have time to focus.

All of the above are ways for you to make your life more effortless. These days, you can get meal kits delivered to your house (so you don't have to go shopping) or have a toilet paper subscription, which is just one less thing to worry about. I know people who have standard outfits and plan what they wear all week, so they don't have to waste precious energy on trying to decide what to wear at 6 am (or have their day ruined before it even really started when they realise that their favourite skirt won't zip up anymore).

Getting organised

Take some time to review the last couple of weeks or so. How much productive time did you actually have and what were some great frustrations. Start with a big brain dump: free up 30 minutes of your time and write down all the things you do, want to do, should do or have to do. For most of you, 30 minutes won't be enough, but we've to start somewhere and I don't want you to put this off because you really need a day or two to capture it all. We'll start with half an hour and get everything you can think of down on paper. In case you're struggling to think of everything, you can capture each of the tasks you're working on in a blank schedule, as you're going through the next week.

Don't limit yourself to 'business' related tasks and actions, but also consider your day job and your household chores. The entrepreneurial life isn't black and white. You can't close your laptop at 5 pm and draw a line in the sand, so you want to look at the big picture and create a life you love and a lifestyle you can sustain longer-term.

Now revisit the list and make the following decisions for each task:

1. Do I want to/have to still do this task in the future? Is it part of my ideal day?
2. Is this task in my zone of genius?
3. Do I have to do it? Can I delegate it or automate it (e.g. delegating making dinner to a spouse or the writing of your blog posts to a copywriter)?
4. How often does this have to be done (e.g. daily, weekly, monthly, etc.)?
5. Can this be prepared in advance (e.g. scheduling of social media posts, ordering the food shop online)?

You can do this in a notebook, on a whiteboard or on a big piece of flipchart paper - whatever works best for you. I would, however, suggest you capture it in an online document at some point so you can work through it and update it in the future, without having to start from scratch. It's like a financial budget, just that you're focusing on time.

The key to creating a successful side hustle without burning out or forcing you to give up your 9-5 before you're ready, is to figure out how you can get everything done in the 168 hours that you get each week. How can you maximise the time you have? Creating consciousness and transparency around this is the first step.

Map out your ideal week

It's time to translate the above advice into practical steps. As I said in the introduction to the chapter, we need to make sure we evaluate what's realistically possible for us. So often, we aim high because we're excited about our ideas and what's to come, and that's great. But if we repeatedly set ourselves up for disappointment, we won't be able to successfully side hustle for long.

One key thing to managing (our own) expectations is to be very clear on when we're not available. I always tell my clients to start mapping out their ideal week or even plan their strategy for the next week by blocking out any times that they know they're not available, e.g. because they have to get the kids ready for school, work their 9-5 or are doing yoga for an hour (yes, commitments made to yourself count). It's about managing the time you ACTU-ALLY have available.

Take a blank weekly schedule and block out any time you're not free to work on your business. Then block out chunks of time that you are available and want to dedicate to your side hustle. Make sure you also consider self-care, date nights and FaceTime with your best friend. I'd always recommend to think of a worst case scenario (e.g. your day job being busy from 9-5) - as long as you have a plan in place of what you want to focus on each week and you have taken care of the minimal viable actions (the ones that keep your business ticking over) then you can just pick up a task should you find yourself with a spare hour.

Define actions

To complete this section, and to ensure you're set up for success, add any actions you want to your to do list or, even better, your task management system. This could be anything like hiring a VA or a copywriter to help with business-related tasks, amending your Outlook calendar to show your working hours as 9-5 rather than 8-6 or choosing and setting up a meal kit subscription. A lot of these little things will make a difference. And I can promise you that it'll be a lot easier to free up 10 or 15 minutes here and there than it'll be to free yourself up for a whole Saturday.

One final bit of advice on time management: It's ok to ask for help. Whether it's asking your partner to cook dinner three times a week because it means you get an extra 30 minutes of focused time or whether it's your friend who collects the kids from school once a week. Remember that this won't always be needed, but that the demands of a business rise and fall. You will have more intense times as you set up or when you're developing a new offering, but you will also have times where you can focus on the more predictable work of 'just' serving your clients.

Feeling resistance?

I appreciate that this may not be the first book on building a business that you've read. In fact, you likely have read several books, have bought a couple of courses and even once hired a coach, but that business of yours is still more of an idea than reality. You know what you want and you know how to get it... so why are you resisting taking that next step? Because I don't want you to read this book and not get any further than another few scribbles in your newest notebook, I want to mention change resistance here before we dive into the real work of modelling your business and then delivering.

Far too often, people get physically sick because they're so unhappy in their job, relationship or general situation. And that sickness? They just accept it and go day to day, allowing life to just happen to them, rather than making life happen for them. They miss opportunities. Remain stuck. Glued to the same spot.

They become so fixated with how things used to be that they fail to see that, now, they are a different person... an individual who needs new things from life. This is a deeply ingrained mindset; but it's one that can be adjusted. It's time to dig far beneath the surface and discover what is holding you back so that you can counteract and move forward - with purpose.

I've been dealing with change resistance in all its forms

for all of my career. There are so many reasons why we're resisting change and I won't go into all of them (don't worry!), but there are a few that you should know about, because you *can* influence them.

Let's start off by making one thing clear; change is exhausting! Plus, we're experiencing changes at a far higher rate than any generation before us. We are expected to deal with them instantly, adapting our lives to the latest twist in our path. Many of these changes, we have little to no influence over; be these in the workplace or at home. Take 2020 and the abundance of changes that were thrown at us from all angles. The uncertainty has been enough to send many into bouts of anxiety and melt-down; we are simply not equipped to deal with such an onslaught of unpredictability. So we protect ourselves. We stick to the ways of life and actions that we know we can rely on. But... What if we learnt to embrace change? What if we stopped putting such a heavy emphasis on planning ahead and instead enjoyed the freedom of thinking on our feet? When you catch yourself holding on to something that really doesn't serve you because you're too worried about the alternative, which is more uncertain, then challenge yourself on this and consider whether the alternative really is as risky as you seem to think. Talk through your thought process with someone else so that you need to verbalise what would happen rather than only ever thinking about it at 3 a.m. as you're staring at the ceiling of your bedroom.

Secondly… Habits. After a while, your routines become automatic. They become habits; easy to implement with minimal effort. And we all want an easy life, right? The problem is, not all habits are good habits. In fact, most of them are pretty damn awful. It's similar to the feeling of control: if you are unhappy and unfulfilled, at least you know what to expect. It may sound like a strange thing to say, but you're in control of your unhappiness - what if something new made you feel even worse? There's a big issue here: this control is a false perception. Because your life is controlling you. When you get to the point where you just accept the lack of joy in your life, you're no longer sat in the driver's seat. Unfortunately, in this same way, our mind doesn't necessarily distinguish between a good and bad habit. If it's easy, then that's the way to go. And even though you know it's a bad habit, the thought of changing it and coming up with a clear plan to rectify the situation feels like far too big of an ask. So you plod along. Imagine how good it would feel to take on a fresh set of AMAZING habits? You know, the ones that take you closer and closer to your dream business and lifestyle. Just remind yourself that whatever feels uncomfortable now will become a habit too before long and will therefore be just as easy as life is now. It's an uncomfortable move to make, but one that will actually allow you to be back in control: and for real, this time.

Your thoughts create your reality... both the positive and the negative. If you want something new for your life, it's going to require a new thought pattern. This leads to uncertainty... and, with it, the all too familiar flutter in your stomach. Because imagining yourself in a totally different situation can be nerve wracking, can't it? It can also be seriously exciting. When you find yourself in this battle between the good and bad, push the nerves to the side. You'll deal with those thoughts later. Now, you've got an empire to build. Make sure you put in place whatever you need to make this happen - a network that will call you out when you're talking negatively, and reminders around your house and workspace to focus on goals and outcomes, rather than worries.

Lastly, another reason for change resistance that you can influence is stress. Our brains are wired in a way that the fear of the unknown feels far more intense and stressful than knowing that what's coming isn't good. This isn't just a 'woo' concept; it's genuine research. And it means we tend to struggle with letting go. Let's compare two scenarios: in the first, you're waiting for a train to an important meeting, only to hear an announcement that the train is cancelled due to failures on the tracks. Sure, you might be wound up. But you accept the situation and come up with a way to deal with it. Perhaps you'll ring them and rearrange, or go home and hold the meeting on video. In the second scenario, the train keeps getting delayed by a minute at a time. You can feel the stress mounting; will you still make it on time? You're desperately trying to figure out if you can speed up the time once you get off the train, praying that there won't be any more delays along the way. This resistance to letting go and planning a new route is the same with unhappiness. Even when you're miserable, you often will get to the point of resignation; you 'may as well just get on with it'. Look deeper: that's no way to live, is it? Once we know something for certain, we get on with it and make it work (as in the example above), so why don't you create this certainty for yourself by making decisions and then implementing them, without constantly going back over them wondering if there are alternatives?

I'm sure it's slowly sinking in that self-awareness is probably the key skill to develop as an entrepreneur. In your business, there's no one above you that can guide you through performance reviews, give you constructive feedback and book you on to the next leadership course. It's down to you now. So when you're stuck or you're not making the progress you were expecting to make, look inside first. Focus on the things that you can influence, change or action.

"The brick walls are there for a reason. The brick walls are not there to keep us out. The brick walls are there to give us a chance to show how badly we want something. Because the brick walls are there to stop the people who don't want it badly enough. They're there to stop the other people."

RANDY PAUSCH

DEFINING YOUR WHY

"Where you are at today has little to do with what happens moving forward."

MARTY FUKUDA

E ven though this chapter is still part of the first section of the book - the section that is focused on setting the scene for success - we're actually starting to work on your business model right now. You will hear me speak about Business Models a lot, when the common advice seems to be to write a business plan as you embark on the entrepreneurial journey, and this is why:

Business plans are several pages long, go into all the

detail, are often over-engineered out of date by the time you hit 'save', but too complex to keep updated.

A business model on the other hand helps you think through your goals, the structure and set up of your business and who you want to work with. You want to make sure your proposition brings you the income and lifestyle you dream of and is doing something you love. However, that doesn't mean you have to turn into the next Jane Austen and write a book. The Dream Business Model I developed is a one page template and focuses on a few key elements:

- What is the end goal = the **vision**
- What would you like your day-to-day to look like = the **dream lifestyle**
- What's the sweet spot of what you're good at, what you're passionate about and what you can get paid for = your **zone of genius**
- How you're translating your zone of genius into an offering = your **income streams**
- Who needs what you have to offer = your **target market**
- Who can support you in making your vision happen = **partners** (this last one is especially important for side hustlers)!

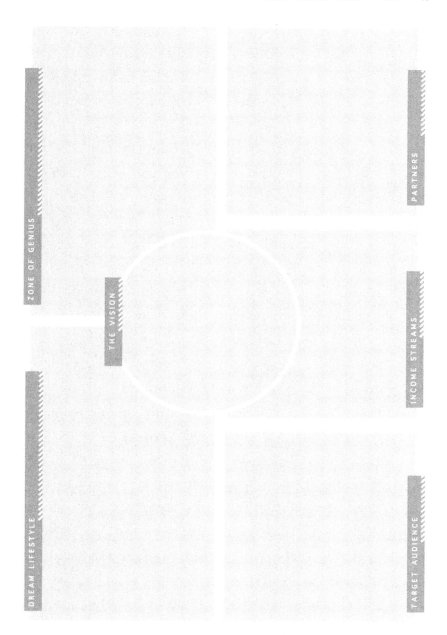

A business model should help you design your entrepreneurial life and help you make key decisions, such as what services or products to offer and how, how to prioritise their development and which opportunities to go after.

Once you are clear on what you want to do, how you want to do it and for whom, then you can dive in deeper and add detail as needed. A business plan can build on the business model for those income streams that may require funding, equity partners, special licences, etc.

I'm giving you this advice for two reasons: Firstly, the world around us changes too quickly and your business model will forever be work in progress as you tweak and adapt to the demands of your clients, react to changes to your circumstances and align it to your evolving dreams. You want to keep complex documentation to a minimum or you'll never look at it again. Secondly, for many of my clients this first step of the process serves as a form of procrastination. They are not moving forward while tweaking and polishing their business plan - adding detail and formatting like champions, but never actually taking action. You need structure and you need to think through the plan, but by keeping it short and precise I'm trying to keep the hurdle as low as possible for you.

As you can see from the outline above, the first two sections of my Dream Business Model are focused on your vision and dream lifestyle - the reason we're thinking about building a business in the first place and the goal we're trying to achieve. Let's start with dreaming big.

Why do I speak about dreaming so much when I'm a practical, outcome-focused person?

Because some of us are better at thinking big and visualisation than others. So, to kick start the process of designing your dream life and business, I invite you to dream. Dreaming is something we all do: at night, when buying that lottery ticket, when watching planes take off at the airport, when we need an escape from the fact that our nose is uncomfortably close to some stranger's arm pit on the Waterloo & City Line at 8:07 am on Monday morning. Also, we limit or censor ourselves less when dreaming. I bet my lovely bluette-coloured (that's a thing) saffiano leather Prada handbag that you looked at some dream houses on Pinterest last time you built a vision board, but then scrolled right on past to the more realistic 5-bedroom new-build that you think you can find on the new development down the road. And lastly, dreaming is a positive experience - you can do it anywhere and anytime. It doesn't require a cork board, scissors and a stack of magazines worth $239.

But don't you worry - we're quickly going to get more practical by translating your dreams into measurable goals.

Creating your vision

"Create a vision for the life you really want and then work relentlessly towards making it a reality."

ROY T. BENNETT

Own up and get clear on what YOU want your life to look like

Taking your dreams and turning them into a vision that you can come back to and call on over and over again is about getting more specific and committing to certain desired outcomes.

A vision is important because it gets you through the hard times. Dreams rarely come true overnight and it's this constant movie running through your head that will keep you going when you are tired, are not sure whether to write that blog post or your weekly newsletter first, and your dog has eaten a whole bar of chocolate so you have to spend the night at the vets. Knowing exactly why you are doing something is one thing, but knowing you are doing something to make your personal dream come true is a game-changer and long-term motivator. It's the one constant in a constantly changing environment where no decision is right or wrong, per se.

As part of your business model, your vision also focuses your actions and decisions. It'll drive your goal-setting and shape your habits and actions - all aligned to get you closer to that dream outcome step-by-step and day-by-day. It will also be easier for you to say yes or no to opportunities by asking yourself whether something will bring you closer to your dream or not. Something would have to be an amazing and fun proposition for you to say "Hell yeah!" despite it not being aligned to your goals - and that's important. It's ok to veer off track as long as you have fun and it's an experience.

You wouldn't believe the number of people who'd roll their eyes at me when I'd share my dream with them (some are more subtle about it than others).

At the risk of sounding like a broken record player (especially if you've been following me for a while): No dream is too big. Or too small. You've probably heard different stories about what the perfect business should look like. About what is expected from you as a coach/photographer/wedding planner/cake designer/list building expert... however, if it doesn't give you butterflies what's the point?

For example, we'd all like more money, but if at the same time you're desperate to only work 4 days a week and 6 hours a day, to spend more quality time with your daughter, then focus on that. That doesn't mean you can't also have more money, but it's a key factor in how you model your dream business (Oh hi there, passive income).

So, make that shiny object syndrome a thing of the past and really focus in on what YOU want your life to look like by translating your dream into a specific, positive and ambitious picture that you can keep at the front of your mind to stay focused.

Formalising your dream

Because you can't hit a moving target, it's important to take that picture in your head and formalise it in some form. It also makes it measurable and transparent - which can be motivating as well as daunting. Being specific is challenging and always makes things more real. Trust me, being uncomfortable is a good thing though. It's the step before growth and breakthrough.

For example, it's much easier to say that you want to launch and grow a Facebook group for your business than it is to say that you want to launch a Facebook group by 31 January and grow it to 500 members by the end of the first year. While the high-level option is easier to come up with, the second option will make it much easier to implement.

Straight away, you can translate the 500 members into monthly targets: i.e. there are 11 months left by the time you launch the group which means you want to gain about 45 members each month. Targets you can then translate into actions, such as sharing the link to your group with your email subscribers or sharing your group on promotional posts in other communities. After a couple of months, you'll know how effective different measures are and you can change what you do (or do more or less of it). So being specific is all about the short-term pain, long-term gain.

You may be really clear on why you're embarking on this journey, or you may want to skip this step and get rid of the headache that all of your ideas are causing you already. I'll be honest: I didn't spend any time on this when I first started. For me it was never a question of whether I would one day have my own business or not - it was a given.

My first memory of entrepreneurship is linked to the wall coming down in Germany. It actually was the car boot sale we organised the day when every citizen of East Germany was entitled to 100 Deutsche Mark welcome money. Did you know that I grew up right on the border? My family and I lived in a small village about an hour outside of Hamburg and from my childhood bedroom on the top floor of the three-storey house, I could see barbed wire fencing and watchtowers marking the border to East Germany in the distance. Between the watchtower and our house was a big field, a meadow, a sandy path, another small meadow, a teeny-tiny beach, and a river. On the other shore of the river was East Germany. Of course, when I was little, we never crossed the river, but it also never occurred to me that I would. So when the borders finally opened, and a ferry service was put in place from the East German side of the river to our little port, our frequent trips across to explore were my first memory of the other side. Back then, we'd still get a stamp in our passports every time we went to visit and who doesn't love a stamp in their passport?

Back to my first entrepreneurial experience though: When Germany was united the year after, East German citizens could collect 100 Deutsche Mark welcome money from our little village post office. Within days, we organised a fete complete with car-boot sale to offer our new neighbours the opportunity to spend their money on things that we really didn't want anymore. Generous, I know. In my case, these were mostly Barbie dolls with horrendous haircuts after my recent 'I-want-to-be-a-hairdresser-phase', completely oblivious to the fact that a doll's hair wouldn't grow back. I was looking forward to shifting some of those ugly things and making some money for new ones.

However, my darling granddad, who had befriended a family that had just made the journey across the river and collected their 100 Deutsche Mark each, told me to give one of the dolls away to the little girl FOR FREE. I was not impressed, but loved my granddad, so complied. Some other business ventures in my childhood years ranged from founding a Mariah Carey fan club and publishing and selling accompanying fanzines in the school playground (illegally as my mother found out from the head teacher eventually), to running small cafes with my brother in our backyard.

Looking back at it now, I don't think I really had a choice but to go down this path I'm on. You will probably feel the same: whether you grew up in an entrepreneurial family, always dreamed of being your own boss and making up your own rules or spent most of your child-hood thinking about what you wanted to be when you grew up and actively prototyped the options, I believe that you were born to be an entrepreneur.

Like I said, I completely missed this step when I first built my business, but instead just started hustling in a way that can loosely be described as throwing spaghetti at the wall to see what sticks. Not very clever. Soon enough I realised that I was doing work I didn't particularly enjoy and in a way that meant I didn't have any more freedom than I did in my corporate roles. Just that the lack of freedom now also came without a regular paycheck or benefits. This is why I had to go back to the drawing board and start again. I had to remind myself why I was on this journey and what my destination was. I'd suggest you do the same.

Start by asking yourself what you *want* to do or be (NOT what you *should* do or be).

I'm explicitly mentioning this so you can make sure you are creating a vision for what you truly desire, not what you want to move away from (positive picture) - a common mistake we make. Don't limit yourself to what you think is realistic and achievable at this point, but think big. Be creative, playful and bold - you can deal with the how later (and I'll help with that)!

Now, get a little more specific. Relax and imagine yourself in this life you want. **What does it look and feel like? What are you doing? Who is there with you and how do you feel about them?**

Write it out. Again: focus on the end-result, not on how you will get there and not on how you will NEVER get there. Because if you want to, you will. Promise!

Now create your vision board. Use pictures and words that get you excited!

Most of you will be familiar with the classic vision board: the cork board above your desk with pictures cut from magazines, that I briefly referred to above. Please tell me I'm not the only one that didn't realise magazines were *this* expensive. The ones with the nice pictures anyway - Conde Nast Traveller, Vogue and Architectural Digest. I love the idea of a vision board, but rarely get around to putting a physical one together. Instead, which I can also highly recommend, I created a PowerPoint slide with pictures from the internet or created a separate, private board on Pinterest. I then saved this as a picture and added it as my desktop background and as a favourite in the photo app on my phone, so I could easily find it and look at it. There are also a number of different apps available that let you create vision boards, set reminders to look at your board daily and add music, etc. to support your visualisation exercise.

Lastly, you could write out your vision. Whether you journal out your dream or create a bullet pointed list of goals, as long as you're documenting it and have the ability to go back and read over it again and again, it's perfect. Writing out your list daily, rather than just reading over it, is something that works really well and may work for you, as long as it's a manageable length. I tried to write down my annual goals twice a day every day earlier this year, which was super powerful, but difficult to maintain. Once a day seems manageable and is a nice start to the day.

Now think of your vision often to keep reminding yourself of what you are striving for. Think of five ways to keep your vision front of mind. For example, think of certain times each day when you could set yourself a reminder to bring up a picture of your vision board, have a picture of it at the front of your notebook or use it as a screensaver for your tablet or laptop. It should be in front of you as often as possible and easily accessible in one form or another in case you feel you need to have a look at it.

Your Dream Lifestyle

"We all have two choices: we can make a living or we can design a life."

JIM ROHN

While your vision will most likely focus on big goals, a state of mind and the people you want to go on this journey with, your dream lifestyle breaks this down into day-to-days practicalities, such as

- what time you want to start and finish work;
- where you'd like to work; and
- what your morning looks like (yoga, journaling, five coffees in the garden?).

By thinking about a typical day in the future, you can come up with goals that you'd like to make happen by building the business.

Your ideal day

I'm about to share an exercise with you that was truly eye-opening for me. I'm probably a first-generation online entrepreneur, and what we saw were people traveling the world and blogging from the beaches of Bali. This freedom, and the independence that came with it, coupled with the technological possibilities, meant that we could virtually (and literally) work from anywhere in the world as long as there was Wi-Fi. Well, and coffee, in my case .

Therefore, when I started thinking of the kind of business I wanted to build, I was thinking of virtual meetings, online courses and all the e-books ('cause passive). This would mean I could in my family's bakery in Germany, eat a piece of cherry and chocolate cake AND MAKE MONEY. Or go to see my friend in Munich whenever I liked and for however long I liked. I could fly to New York to have a Don Ruben Omelette and Pancakes for brunch at 'Sundays in Brooklyn' while working.

Don't get me wrong, I'm still all about brunch in New York and coffee and cake in Germany. That bit hasn't changed. But now I know I also want to do different things: I want a team that I can brainstorm ideas with, work in a coworking space surrounded by other inspiring entrepreneurs and lots of chatter (for some reason, I'm most productive in coffee shops). I want face-to-face client contact regularly. The longer I reflected on this, the more I realised that one of my favourite things in business is the energy I feel when people come together.

For my business this means, I don't want to be all virtual and passive. For me, this means including a face-to-face mini-intensive session to kick off the process whenever I work with new clients on a one-to-one basis and it's logistically possible. I'm thinking about in-person events and retreats - just that they'll be in New York and Hamburg, so I can still have my favourite brunch. In fact, I'll host one in Dubai too!

One of the biggest advantages of running your own business is that you can design it exactly the way you want. Not that it'll always go to plan, but no point settling on something that doesn't feel right, because then you may as well have stayed in your corporate role with someone else paying your private health insurance. And no, for a side hustle, it'll take that little bit longer to get there, but you don't want to start building a business and scale it to 6-figures and beyond, to then pivot like Ross in Friends when you finally have the option to leave your 9 - 5.

I first came across this exercise in a programme by Denise Duffield-Thomas, so this is not one I can take credit for, BUT it is so much fun and the right level of focus when thinking about what your dream life would look like and what you're going on this (sometimes tiring and exhausting) journey for.

Take some time to write about your ideal day and go into as much detail as possible when describing

- your surroundings as you wake up and what time it is;
- how you spend your morning;
- when you start work and what time you finish;
- what you do and how you feel as you go through your day; as well as
- who is with you and what they are doing.

Take some time to complete this exercise and remember that nothing is set in stone. Your circumstances will change which means you'll wish to work from home more or less at times, etc. Maybe go away and daydream a little, be honest about what makes you feel good and what makes you feel drained, lonely and isolated. Don't over-think it, and have a little fun with this!

Defining your lifestyle goals

Once you completed the Ideal Day exercise you'll have a pretty good idea of what your ideal day looks like, which will be key when you're getting stuck into building a life and business that works for YOU. Of course, it'll be more complex to manage if you dream of having a team and most of your work is based on 1:1 time with clients, BUT if that is what you enjoy the most, then it's worth it.

Right now, you're laying the foundation for your future, so pull out some of the key themes you want to achieve through building the business, such as "want to work from an office", "want to finish at 3 pm to spend the afternoon with the kids" or "want to see at least one client face-to-face each day". List them out as your more short-term goals and then highlight a few of those that you can achieve while running your side hustle and still working your 9-5, because this will play a role when you start building and implementing your idea and need to make decisions about how you'd like to run the operations of your business. Yes, that's right. You mean business now and that comes with running operations and a back-office. It's less daunting than it sounds though, I promise!

Something to watch out for…

Goals are amazing and, quite frankly, we need something to aim for because it's impossible to hit a moving target. However, they can often have the opposite effect because, in all of our excitement, we are too optimistic.

A new idea, coupled with my lack of patience and the buzz of potential, is my ruin. In my mind, I think I can work all night and weekend to make it happen when, in reality, I tend to go to bed at 9 pm because I have a baby.

No, scrap that - I'm not going to use her as an excuse - I've always loved an early night.

But it's demoralising, isn't it? Clearly defining those goals and never reaching them? Instead, what you should do is to plan for the most exhausted version of yourself in line with my mantra 'underpromise and overdeliver'. I'm saying that because aiming low doesn't mean you can't deliver more than planned should you find yourself with an hour or two to spare (imagine it... it's like a dream), and it also doesn't mean it'll take forever. Taking small steps consistently will add up, and we're actually more focused if and when we only have limited time available. We will cover this in much more detail later in the book!

Be kind to yourself. Make the goals realistic but fluid.

Something else we'll cover a little later on is why setting short-term goals is more likely to bring you long-term success and how to organise your days and weeks to make them happen.

ACTION PLAN

Y ou're at the end of the first section of the book and by now you should know:

- that you're meant for more and should go after this dream of yours;
- what your big vision looks like; and
- what your dream lifestyle means for you, day-to-day ,and what it'll take to make it happen.

Because I'm a sucker for ticking things off a list, I'm including a list of actions you should complete at the end of each section:

1. Find three ways to free up time in your working week.

2. Map out your ideal week to get clear on how much time you have to spend on this project.
3. Create and document your vision.
4. Outline your dream lifestyle and translate that into clear goals.

In the next section, we're going to dive right into how you can make your side hustle happen, so that your vision will be your reality one day.

2
_____

MODEL

O nce you're clear on the direction you're taking, the next step is to come up with a plan of how to get there, and this is exactly what the second section of this book is about.

We'll be looking at exactly what it'll take to make your vision and dream lifestyle a reality: from finding out which of your strengths and skills you want to leverage in your business, to the different ways you're going to make money and why your clients should work with you and not one of the alternative providers in your space (consciously not using the word competitor here because you're unique and therefore don't need to compete for your ideal client).

We'll define that target market you want to work with to make sure they can pay you, are accessible for you and there are enough of them to achieve the kind of revenue you need. Lastly, we'll identify who you'll need on your team to deliver this long-term.

At the end of this section, I want you to have a clear picture of what your business is going to look like, ready to plan and implement!

IDENTIFYING YOUR ZONE OF GENIUS

"If you are human, you have a calling: to live your genius."

GAY HENDRICKS

The preparations are done and it's finally time to get down to business. You've worked out that you (absolutely) can do it, when you might be able to do it and why you want to build this business. The logical next step is to figure out what you'll be doing.

One major hurdle to building your dream business is finding the right idea. Those with an entrepreneurial mind often have lots of ideas: Services or products they've used that they know could have been better, a talent that they'd love to monetise, or a gap in the market that they've worked in for years that's frustrated them.

The number one reason we start a business is to create a better, more balanced life and have more time to do the things we love. Often, we make the decision when we're at breaking point: redundancy, burnout, that third and unexpected child on the way, the fourth time we've been overlooked for the promotion we'd deserve, and apparently a pandemic.... Not having time to prepare, save money or start your business as a side hustle means you have to act quickly to be able to pay the bills, which is why many entrepreneurs start a business based on their previous career or a beloved hobby.

What's the problem with that?

Nothing.

IF you're passionate about it...

AND...

It aligns with your dream lifestyle!

Starting a business that simply replaces the 9 - 5 you left behind, but offers you no benefits, a lot more responsibilities and no chance to switch off (hi there, 7-day week) is not what you dream off, right?

However, the most common problem I come across when working with my clients is that we feel we have to stay in the lane we've been in most of our career, even though there's a reason why we were fed up with it, that goes beyond the commute and the annoying boss. I was in this camp, following that Monday morning when I quit my job, which I told you about in the introduction. I had to come up with a plan quickly as I didn't have savings in the bank to pay my bills for a while, while I figured things out. I didn't have a business plan worked out. I hadn't even thought of the right idea. But I knew I wasn't going to look for another permanent role that would leave me frustrated because I'd give more than I'd ever get out of it.

Because I had to move quickly, I decided to stay in the space I was in and use my experience to win clients. I'd worked as a Programme and Change Manager most of my life, so I updated my CV (the most painful process known to man) and sent it to some former managers and contacts that worked in businesses that would likely need the kind of help I could offer. Within a week, I had secured my first 6-month contract. The pressure was off. I could take a deep breath, pay my rent, buy food and figure out what I'd be doing longer-term.

Finding myself in that corporate space again, looking after a huge project that was critical to the business, I knew I had so much to offer to make this better for companies. I started working on a proposition and business aimed at big corporate clients, hired a designer to come up with a brand identity and wrote pages and pages of copy for my website. But before I knew it, the excitement wore off quickly, as I found myself on the commuter train into The City, or stuck at Waterloo station because of an 'incident' between Clapham Junction and Vauxhall, with thousands of other people desperate to get home. This is exactly what I didn't want to do anymore. Mind you, I wanted to be in London, but not all day and not at the times that meant I had to almost sit on someone else's lap, or listen to them chew their tuna and onion sandwich loudly on the train. The onion alone would have been bad enough without any sound effects! How had I gotten this so wrong?

That's my story and it obviously doesn't have to be like that. You may feel very passionate about your profession, but you may want to make more of an impact than you're able to as part of the corporate machine. This could be serving a different target audience that isn't 'interesting' (=profitable) enough for your employer. Or perhaps you want to pursue more radical ideas and disrupt the space you're in. Or, and this is often the case, you want to start making money for yourself rather than someone else - especially if that someone else doesn't value you nearly as much as they should. I've shared my story with you above, because I want to challenge you and make sure you do what you do for the right reason. I don't want you to spend a lot of effort and money to go down one path, when it's not the right one. I learned that lesson so that you don't have to.

Alternatively, we turn a hobby into a business: It's

something we enjoy, we're often very good at it and the fact that our family and friends are all asking us to make their cakes/Christmas wreaths/design their living room gives us the idea that it's something we could make money doing. But we soon fall out of love with it when it's not the therapeutic process that we enjoyed so much anymore, but now comes with the pressure of it having to pay the bills and customers asking for refunds, even though we've already bought all the ingredients or supplies to deliver their order.

When considering this path, it's very important to carefully consider the time for money formula: How long does it take you to create your product or deliver your service and how much would a potential client pay for the output.

For example, I'm a baker's daughter and know how much time it takes to make a 5-tier wedding cake with lots of intricate detail. It takes hours and hours. Does anyone want to pay for it? No. The budget is usually more aligned to the idea of a bunch of donuts. Or writing: I love to write - it's definitely my favourite creative outlet. So every now and again, I wonder if I could offer copywriting services. Until I wrote this book. While I can still create my own schedule and I don't have a client breathing down my neck and tapping their fingers on the table next to me, I still have a deadline that's in the not-too-distant future and I know the output isn't just for me. So, while it's still something I enjoy, it feels different.

It's great if you can monetise a hobby and talent, but it's also ok to have something you're incredibly good at and do it just for you. Sometimes, that's hard to remember, because once you're in the entrepreneurial mindset, you see opportunities everywhere and want to pursue them.

Lastly, if you're toying with an idea based on your experience with a service that is missing something which you know you can add, then this is the best scenario. Even more so, if it's something you're passionate about (which it often is, which is also why we spend more time thinking about this service specifically, rather than about other things that could be improved). The only call out here is to be clear on what it'll take to deliver this and whether it's something you can do on your own. While business partners make things more complex and it takes more admin to get started, it also can really accelerate your go-to-market time and reduce your costs. If, for example, you want to build an app and need an app developer, it may be sensible to find a partner as you'll always need to improve the technology, fix bugs, respond to issues raised by customers, etc. You can outsource this, but then you're always relying on a third party, which is risky too. As with a lot of decisions in business (and life for that matter), there's no right or wrong, but it very much depends on your situation and proposition.

Your zone of genius

The best place to start defining your business model, and focus in on your business idea, is your zone of genius. But what exactly is it? It's not necessarily the profession you have the most experience in, it doesn't have to be what you have three different certifications in and it's definitely not the thing that you think you SHOULD be doing (because 'should' almost always implies external (if well-meant) influence by people that don't have to live your life and with the consequences of your actions).

When I speak about identifying your zone of genius, what I mean is:

discovering what you love + what you're good at = your purpose.

But that's not all of it. In a business context, we need to add in an extra variable to narrow down your zone of genius:

What you love + what you're good at + what you can get paid for = your zone of genius.

As you can see, we're already dipping our toes into your business proposition and possible income streams here, so before we do that, I want to take a step back and focus in on your mad skills (as some would say).

Let's set the scene real quick here, because I often speak about my slightly different understanding of strengths and weaknesses with my clients and I want you to bear this in mind too, as we're tackling your zone of genius.

For me, a strength is not (necessarily) something you're good at, but rather something you enjoy doing which gives you energy. A weakness on the other hand is something you may or may not be good at, but doing it drains you. When something drains you it translates into procrastination and exhaustion. It's not the first time I've said it and it won't be the last: Building a business isn't easy. It's really hard work at times, so you ABSOLUTELY want to make sure you're doing something you enjoy!

I often give the example of my hatred of writing project plans. I find it soul-destroying. In fact, I'd seriously consider getting a root canal treatment over writing another project plan. Considering that I spent most of my career so far as a programme manager, that may come as a surprise to some of you and you may wonder why I hate something that's such a key element in my profession. And rightly so. Here's why: I spent most of my career managing very complex, global, multi-functional change projects for huge organisations. Of course those organisations wanted me to write project plans. All-encompassing plans of all activities that had to happen across the world in the next 18 - 24 months. Breaking everything down into tasks, grouping them together into sensible packages, putting due dates against them and assigning them to someone (other than myself - oh, the feeling of authority and power). BUT I hate it, because guess what happened EVERY SINGLE TIME? The plan was out-of-date before I could move my cursor to the top left corner of my screen to hit 'save' . Whether the scope changed, a market in scope moved out of scope or a technology team raised a risk around user acceptance testing that now needed an extra three weeks in at least 80% of the countries, something always shifted. Daily. And if there's anything I hate, it's waste. Waste of time and effort in this case. Why produce something you very well know will change almost immediately? I could rant about this all day, but that's not why you bought this book. However, I wanted to share this example to show you that something you're good at (I'm good at planning and can write these plans in my sleep) can drain you and therefore shouldn't be considered a strength. And it should even less be something that you build your business doing.

I want you to remember this as you're working through some of the steps that I'm about to suggest you do to narrow down your zone of genius. Challenge your own thinking to figure out whether something you're good at and something you may have been doing all of your life is actually something that you LOVE doing. Whether it's something that makes you jump out of bed in the morning.

Step 1: Research

This first step is about reflecting on your personal and professional history and looking back at some key moments in your life as they give you invaluable insights into what your strengths are, what you feel passionate about and what gives you joy. I want you to find the things that make you smile and leave you buzzing. Think of those meetings that you walk out of with a spring in your step - what did you do? Remember that time you forgot to drink coffee and you accidentally only had four cups that day because you were so absorbed in what you were doing? This is what I'm talking about.

(By the way - that coffee thing is crazy. Has happened to me once. I still call myself a willpower ninja...)

Start by listing all the things that you love and care about. Consider those things that would make you get out of bed at 4 am to be able to do it. Or that thing that frustrates and irritates you so much that you desperately want to change it.

Then create a list of all the things you're good at. Getting more difficult, right? Start with those things you have experience in and think about your transferable skills. Yes, I can plan a big project (not necessarily relevant to all entrepreneurs), which also means that I can break down and structure complex problems - something that's needed in all sorts of professional settings. Spend some time going in deeper and figuring out those skills you can transfer to a new profession - it'll be worth it. But also add the things that your friends always ask you to help them with. Depending on how self-critical you are, this little exercise could be really hard work. If you struggle to think of things, then I want you to ask for help. Ask former colleagues, co-workers or friends for feedback on why they enjoy or enjoyed working with you and what they value most about you. It's a step out of the comfort zone for most of us, but I have done it before and actually appreciated all the comments I got back, and they have helped me immensely. In case your impostor gremlin has started shouting at you as you're reading this paragraph: You are asking for your strengths, so none of them have to think you are perfect, just give their view of what you do best. I'm enclosing a template email below - feel free to copy and use this!

———

Template Email

Hey there!

This is going to a small number of people that I respect and trust (that's YOU) — and I promise, this won't take more than a moment of your time.

I'm doing some personal development at the moment and my coach has challenged me to find out my 3 strongest qualities. I'm really curious to hear your take, because it is so hard to do this on my own.

From the outside looking in, what do you believe are my 3 best, strongest qualities? What do you come to me for or where do you see me offering substantial value to others?

Please hit reply and let me know. Of course, I'll be the only one to see what you write.

I know you're really busy, so if you don't have the time, I totally understand.

But if you're able to share anything, it would help me tremendously. I really value and respect your opinion and your time.

Thank you ever so much,
[Your name]

———

While you don't want to stay in the corporate space, you can think back to performance reviews and promotions.

Try and remember why you got certain jobs and responsibilities, which of those you enjoyed and why.

Creating these lists is not a 30-minute exercise. While it can sometimes be helpful to set a timer to create that 'fake' deadline and force outputs (for those deadline dancers among us), these lists are going to grow with time. Allow them to. Just because you're offering something in your business today, doesn't mean you can't add something else into the mix next year. You have to start somewhere, but business models evolve over time, just like we do.

Step 2: Model

Now that you have two lists (or the beginning of two lists), you can start having fun. It's time to connect the dots. The exercise above should give you plenty of ideas and material for this next step, in which I want you to combine some of the above to narrow down your zone of genius.

To do this, go through the lists and play around with a few combinations. You want to pick something you're passionate about and something you're good at, such as the example below:

Women feeling confident in a business context (passion) + product design (strength)

or

Animal welfare (passion) + content creation (strength)

You may have several passions and you'll likely have a huge amount of strengths, so there are lots and lots of combinations you can come up with. As above, list them all out for now without editing yourself (yet). See how you feel as you come up with them - excited, curious, bored?

Note: Just because you've been doing something for 15 years in your career and you're amazing at it, doesn't mean you have to love it. Feeling bored with something you're good at is ok and you're doing the right thing of finding alternatives with this exercise. Trust me, it's better to find out that you're not excited about something now rather than two years down the line when you have spent an immense amount of time and effort on building a business that gets you about as excited as another three-day process design workshop with the IT Team (no offence to any of business process consultants out there - I used to be you!).

Now we're definitely at a point where things get really, REALLY exciting: we're talking specific business ideas! Work your way through all your combos from the exercise above and add as many ideas for services (or even products) for each of the combinations that you've listed previously as you can think of. It'll be much easier to come up with ideas for combinations that you love than it will for combinations that you can do, but may not feel excited about - so listen to your intuition. Don't force anything, but trust the process and use it to further narrow down your zone of genius.

Picking up the examples I used previously, here are some ideas:

Women feeling confident in a business context (passion) + product design (strength) = merchandise with inspirational quotes

or

Animal welfare (passion) + content creation (strength) = social media management for dog walkers or companies producing vegan products

After a couple (ok, three) failed business attempts, I finally realised that I had to go back to the drawing board and start again, and this is when I came up with this process that I'm sharing with you. While I could use my vast experience managing complex programmes for corporates, I really didn't feel passionate about it. Not only did I not feel passionate about it, but I also didn't have the freedom or flexibility to work from anywhere in the world (or at least from Germany when seeing my family more). With my next business idea, I was doing something that I felt really, really passionate about and that finally allowed me to work from anywhere but I didn't use my strengths at all. Next up, I tweaked my proposition to use more of my strengths while working flexibly and there definitely was a huge need for what I had to offer, but my oh my, yet again I didn't feel excited about what I was doing whatsoever. So far, I had tweaked my proposition on the fly over and over again, just tweaking my copy to reflect the new direction I was taking. To be honest, at this point I just felt tired and exhausted and as though I clearly wasn't cut out for entrepreneurship. The fact that I'd just found out that I was pregnant, spent the majority of my days in the bathroom with "morning" sickness (I'm pretty sure it was a male doctor with a twisted sense of humour that named this), while suffering from some serious caffeine withdrawal and a persistent (pre-Covid) cough, probably didn't help my level of confidence.

BUT this change in my personal circumstances also motivated me to not give up yet. I knew I had to finally get it right. So rather than tweaking my proposition mid-flight again, I took a step back and started from scratch, going through the exact process that I'm sharing with you here: I started right at the end (i.e. my vision and dream lifestyle).

As I was working through what I wanted from life, I realised that one of the things I feel really passionate about is entrepreneurship and business ideas. I love when women around me dreamed big and took giant leaps. One of my strengths is to break down big, complex projects and problems, provide some structure, define actions and hold people accountable while they are moving closer to the big outcome, step-by-step. I'm good at finding solutions and showing the way one can get there.

· · ·

Entrepreneurship (passion) + solutions and planning (strengths) = Business Model Strategy and Implementation

I wanted to share my personal story with you to show you what it can look like and how things you do, have done or want to do can be tailored to something you feel passionate about. If I felt more passionate about travelling, for example, I could have looked into travel design. If I was more passionate about women overcoming their anxiety (which I am passionate about, but not as qualified to work on), I could have looked at life coaching.

Same as above: Make a start but don't feel like you HAVE TO define a million-dollar-business idea right now. These are ideas that we'll take forward into the next chapter on income streams to define what your actual product or service could and will look like.

PROPOSITION AND INCOME STREAMS

"Make the money, don't let the money make you. Change the game, don't let the game change you."

MACKLEMORE.

This is the piece of the puzzle that brings together everything we've spoken about so far, and this is where so many business models go wrong. It's time to determine whether an idea is in alignment with your vision and dream lifestyle and whether the ideas are based in your zone of genius.

But before we dive into that, I want to clear something

up that's very close to my heart: you should never, ever just have one income stream, but a minimum of two to three. The world around us is changing too quickly for us to put all our eggs in one basket! And it's not just about de-risking your business (and life!). It also means that you get to have more variety - I know us entrepreneurial types are bursting with ideas and it'd be a shame to have to choose just one (and get bored quickly).

I'm sure it's no surprise to you that a lot of the entrepreneurs I've been speaking to recently, who have lost all or at least a huge chunk of their income when the pandemic hit, were focusing their energy on just one income stream. This could have been retail in a brick-and-mortar setting, travel consultancy, event management or catering or beauty services to name a few. Their businesses had to shut overnight and not everyone was set up to move online and, to be honest, it doesn't make sense in every industry or all the circumstances. I'm not saying that to accuse anyone for not being prepared, for missing opportunities or for not thinking big enough. No one saw this coming and even less so the extent of it. I've been managing complex, global change programmes for over 15 years and never once have I seen 'a pandemic' on the risk log! However, now that we know, we know, and it's only responsible to make sure we take this into consideration when designing our business model.

Now it may also make more sense to you why I previously told you not to restrict yourself when it comes to business ideas and keeping an open mind when it comes to the possible combinations in your zone of genius. Sometimes, the smartest thing you can do is not to limit yourself to just one industry or area of expertise!

Let's have a quick look at your overall proposition before we go into the design of your income streams and then choosing the one you want to launch your business with (**EXCITING!!!**).

An Introduction to Proposition Design

To be straight to the point: your business proposition outlines the reason why your customer should buy from, or pay you instead of someone else. It's about understanding how you're different to other, similar businesses on the market (I consciously don't use the term competitors here), why you're different and how this makes a difference to your customers or clients.

This goes beyond just taking one of your ideas and designing what that looks like. It allows you to think a bit bigger and consider what you and your business stand for. Ultimately, a business is successful when it relieves an acute pain for a customer (group) in a way that is easy and accessible (opposed to solving a problem, but it being so complicated that the barrier for the customer to engage is too high and they don't see that you're the one that can help them - something that is a problem more often than you'd think). You want to be clear about what you provide to your customer or clients and how this helps them do their job better. BUT it's also where you can add in your unique experience, expertise and what you feel passionate about.

If you're passionate about animal welfare and you want to support a charitable cause by donating a percentage of your profits, then this could be unique to you and may be the deciding factor when a client chooses you over another entrepreneur with a similar offering. You'll probably have come across the term USP - Unique Selling Proposition, before and this is not much different. Your proposition is very personal to you and therefore can also be referred to as your Unique Value Proposition.

These are some of the questions you can think through as you're considering your UVP:

- Is there anyone other than your clients that you want to provide value to (e.g. your employees, your partners, your suppliers, a charitable cause, etc.)?
- What are some of the things your customer can't live without and can you include any of this in your services?
- What can you do to simplify the life and/or work of your customer?
- What are some of the challenges that your

customers face when working with a business in your sector?

- Do you or your service give your customer something that they wouldn't expect and that will add surprise? Could you?
- Does it reduce some of the risks that your customers are afraid of and are trying to mitigate?

Don't forget that this is the stuff that makes your business personal to you and also shapes the way you can surprise and delight your customers. I promise you, the nicest thing about being in business are the messages of gratitude you receive from clients that are telling you how excited they are to be working with you. With YOU!

I wanted to give you this introduction to creating your proposition before we dive into defining your income streams as this will help you to actively design them.

An introduction to income streams

Your income streams are the different sources that generate revenue for your business, but don't have to be limited to just your business (think property). Building a side hustle, by nature, is a second income stream while you're still earning an income from a corporate role - so you're well on your way to the two to three income streams I recommend you have.

If you've spent any time researching business ideas and devouring resources on how to start a business of your own, you will have heard a lot of talk about passive income. It seems as though passive income is the holy grail of the online business world, so I want to cover it here, but also with a warning: Passive income is only passive once you've done all the hard work of putting the income stream in place.

There are a number of different passive income opportunities out there and they take various degrees of work to set up, manage and maintain. I will run through some examples below.

(Semi-) Passive Income Streams

Digital products: E-books, downloadable templates or resources, stock photography or online courses are some of the digital products that have been hailed as great passive income opportunities, BUT they take a lot of work to create in the first place. Going through the process of writing this book, I can confirm that writing an e-book is not passive and not a laughing matter (and I love writing). Same goes for online courses and any kind of downloadable tools, templates or resources. Mapping out the content, writing the content, creating the assets and resources (such as videos and workbooks) and making these available on a platform takes time, mental capacity and a lot of effort. Depending on how you deliver, for example, a course, this could also be classed as semi-passive income. If you deliver the training live on a weekly basis, then this obviously still means you have to show up, but you show up for an hour and teach ten, twenty, thirty, four hundred people rather than serving a client one-to-one.

However, it's not just the product itself, but also the sales funnel that goes with it. By default, you'll want to design an automated process that you take your customer through (otherwise it won't be passive, right?) and that takes a lot of input too. From building an audience, to writing and designing sales pages and setting up payment integrations, building a funnel can take time and a lot of copy. Trust me, no one ever tells you that copywriting is THE key skill when running an online business! I will tell you more about building funnels in the third section of the book that is focused on implementation, but wanted to make sure I mention it here, before you design an all-passive business proposition because you heard 'passive is massive' or something like that. (By the way, I think I just came up with that phrase and am now seriously considering buying the domain...)

Affiliate marketing and referrals: Becoming an affiliate or referring business to trusted business partners is another way to make passive income. This can be anything from registering as an affiliate for online retailers and applications, to becoming an affiliate for programmes run by entrepreneurial peers. The expectation is that you recommend their products, programmes or business in general and share your unique link alongside it, so that people can sign up and you get paid for the referral.

If you truly love a product or service and would recommend it, then this is a great way to make additional income, however dropping links in the odd social media post and email newsletter will not result in payments covering your mortgage (or even your weekly Friday night takeaway) unless your audience is huge. Affiliate schemes for online courses are a lot more profitable, but the sale is much harder too, considering the investment. It requires a lot more time and effort to create social media content, email sequences, online interviews with the coach, etc. This can potentially also distract from your message, so you want to make sure the timing is right and doesn't interfere with your own course or product launches. So much to think about, right?

Memberships and subscriptions: These are the last models I want to introduce and discuss here. Offering an online business membership means that you have monthly revenue coming in from a large number of people who in turn have access to a database of content, exclusive training (delivered by yourself or third parties) and networking with other business owners. As you can see, this is a semi-passive income stream as you'll have to still continuously provide content and training, etc. or people would consume the content and leave, but of course there's no limit to the number of people that could technically join the membership, which can be a very substantial monthly income for you.

Other formats that fit the membership model are networking groups, peer boards or masterminds. Again, it's like your sports club or gym (where you have access all the time), but without the sweat or guilt (it's always one or the other for me).

I'm sure you're all familiar with subscription models, but I want to include them here for completeness. These can range from subscriptions for software and applications all the way to co-working spaces (so 2019, I know). Anything that you can give your clients access to on a month-by-month basis works for this!

Reading the above may make you think that I'm not a fan of (semi-)passive income, but that's not true. I think that every entrepreneur should have several passive income streams because it's the best thing in the world to make money while you sleep. BUT I've highlighted some of the challenges, because the creation and management of those income streams is anything but passive. It takes a lot of time and effort to build an audience big enough to make a decent amount of money from this, considering that traditional conversion rates are between 1% and 3% (5% if you're a copywriting superstar). If you then consider the time and effort required to build the product and funnel as well as the work involved in managing this funnel (this could be anything from keeping content up-to-date, helping people log in or dealing with refund requests, etc.), it isn't as passive as you would imagine. It's all worth it, but go into this with your eyes wide open.

However, as I said, including these income streams in your business model is a must and allows you to move away from trading time for money in a setting where you're serving one client at time.

Traditional Income Streams

Brick-and-mortar: This category includes your traditional shops and beauty salons, but also hotels, restaurants and co-working spaces. I don't often see this in the side hustle space, but wanted to list it as an opportunity. Of course you could open a brick-and-mortar business and staff it so that you don't actually have to be there running it, but that's rare. Knowing what we know now (thanks 2020), we would approach this with more caution and if you're looking at opening a brick-and-mortar retail outlet, then I'd consider an omni-channel approach with an online presence.

Person-to-person and Events: Person-to-person

services are coaching, training, holistic treatments and teaching in any shape or form. These services can be delivered for one person or alternatively through an event, which means training, workshops, retreats or conferences. Of course, traditionally, these take place in-person, at restaurants or hotels, but most or all of these can also be hosted virtually now. This allows you to attract a more global audience and is very cost-effective, but also needs to be designed differently and certain aspects of it may not translate to a virtual environment.

Online retail or services: It feels as though there may be an overlap to some of the passive income examples I included above, but there are a number of propositions that include product sales and virtual services, that are not necessarily captured so far. This can be having an online shop (without the brick-and-mortar sidekick) or supporting business owners as a Virtual Assistant, Online Business Manager or any other supportive function. For me, this also includes freelance or contract-based roles, so taking on an interim role with an (often) corporate organisation with the aim to deliver a specific piece of work or project.

The list I've shared is by no means complete and there are more variations and possibilities out there. I wanted to show you some of the options that are quite common as it very much depends on your personal preference, and the vision you defined for yourself, how you choose to work.

Think about how you like to serve your clients, what settings inspire and motivate you and then tailor your offering to this. This is the reason why I ask you to define your vision, dream lifestyle and identify your zone of genius first - before we even start thinking about what your business is going to look like.

For me personally, this meant that I have created a bespoke coaching offer that allowed me to combine different ways of serving my clients. I love the energy of in-person meetings (just not where they often happen: boring, beige rooms with chairs that have questionable stains on them), so I want to meet my clients face-to-face in beautiful hotel lobbies or restaurants for an initial mini-intensive lasting 2-3 hours. However, I also want to be able to work from my mom's spare room or the coffee shop near my best friend's house in Germany and not have to get on a train every day (because I don't really like them much even during off-peak hours) to go into London, so after the initial in-person meeting, we work together virtually unless it makes sense to get together in person again.

As you can see, you can absolutely tailor it to your needs, style and dream lifestyle. Keep that in mind as we're moving on to the next part about mapping out YOUR income streams and deciding which service you want to launch with.

Mapping out your income streams

I'll suggest you look at this part of your business model from two angles: (1) decide which two to three (as a minimum) income streams you'd like to build, and then (2) decide which one you want to focus on and launch first. One of my mentors put it well the other day when she said that you can absolutely do everything, but not at the same time. This is even more true when you are starting and running your business on a part-time basis.

As you start out, you want to focus your energy on developing one core offer - a product or service that you can deliver alongside your 9 - 5.

To get started, I want you to revisit the product and service ideas that you came up with in the last chapter and list out up to five that you feel excited about. Now consider the following questions to narrow down your launch idea further:

- What is your experience in the subject matter?
- How passionate do you feel about the idea?
- Do you have resources available to launch this product or could you create these quickly and effortlessly?
- How profitable could this idea be? What's the profit margin like?

Use the information you come up with to create a short list of two to three ideas and options that you want to take forward and work on in more detail.

Shortlist:

1. _____
2. _____
3. _____

In this next step, I want you to flesh out these ideas to consider the format of how you're planning to work with your clients, the deliverables included and the price point.

The What

When it comes to the ways you wish to work with your clients, you should really focus in on what works for you, what you find most fun about your work and what it would take for your clients to achieve a successful outcome, especially when you're offering coaching, teaching or treatments. This means you may want to meet with them for an hour every week to progress quickly, or, if you need them to have more time to implement in between sessions, you may want to only meet them every other week or even once a month. Decide whether you want to speak to them on Zoom or meet them in person, and also how much access they have to you in between meetings, because it's important to set boundaries.

Below you can see what I've included in my 1:1 coaching offer:

Detailed questionnaire – First, my clients fill out a detailed intake questionnaire so I can understand where in the process they are at, what their circumstances are and what they are hoping to achieve in our time together.

One 3-hour intensive – During this intensive, we'll agree goals for the business and our time together, and map out steps to get there.

Two 1-hour coaching calls per month – We'll use these calls to dive deeper into their progress and to "course-correct" their plan as needed. These are also important for accountability.

Two 15-minute S.O.S. calls – If a client needs some extra support between sessions, they're covered!

One 1-Hour Mindset Coaching Session - My client will get a 60-Minute coaching with a mindset coach to unlock any blocks or limiting beliefs.

Individualised action plans between sessions – This will be tailored to my client's needs. Example homework assignments include: Definition of services, creation of assets, creation of marketing channels, etc.

Done for you funnel - My team builds a funnel for my client, so they can start/continue building their audience.

Unlimited email and Voxer access between coaching calls because I know that the best ideas and the big questions come to my clients while they're walking their dog on a Sunday afternoon.

Try and think through what it would take for your client to achieve their goals and make sure that's covered. I know that every one of my clients struggles with their mindset at one point or another, so I'm collaborating with another coach to make sure they have an hour that they can use anytime they feel they need it, while we're working together. It's included in the price and I pay for this (but because it's a collaboration, I get preferential rates). I also include the work of building their funnel, because I know that the technical set up of this can feel overwhelming when you first start out and it's yet another popular reason to procrastinate.

The How

This is where your desired lifestyle comes into the mix as well as your zone of genius. While there was a huge trend of working completely virtually for maximum (geographical) flexibility, I soon figured out that I love the face-to-face contact with my clients and need the energy of an in-person meeting to stay motivated and inspired. On the flip side, I work with clients from all over the world, so regular meetings aren't always possible. As I mentioned before, my compromise is that I try and meet my clients in person for the initial 3-hour intensive, before we then move to regular meetings on Zoom.

Of course, there are different considerations here, especially when looking at side hustling: How can you make this work to fit in with your schedule and around your 9 - 5? Would the idea enable you to implement your dream lifestyle? Of course, we may not be able to go all in when it comes to lifestyle, but it's important to move in the right direction and to try and implement some elements of it, so you know why you're doing this and for balance.

Again, consider your clients needs too and figure out how you can support them best. You'll be able to come back to this and refine it once you're clearer on your target market.

The Price

Pricing a service is a tricky business, and a real mindset challenge, especially when we first start out and don't really have a benchmark. We tend to look at entrepreneurs that offer services and products that are similar to ours and then the impostor syndrome kicks in. Of course, *they* can charge that amount because they have ALL the experience and have been doing this for a minimum of 198 years and their website is so professional. No one would pay me that much. Or would they?

They would actually. Those people that need and value what you offer will pay you what you deserve. You don't charge them for the 60 minutes a week you spend with them, nor do you charge them for the experience you've gained working with clients since you set up shop three weeks ago. They pay you for

- the university degree that you studied three years for,
- the three professional qualifications you got while working full-time too,
- the 10+ years you spent making someone else a lot of money and
- they pay you for your unique point-of-view and life experience.

However, I get that you also want to have the opportunity to test and refine your offers while getting some valuable testimonials for your website and a lot of coaches recommend offering your services for free initially. I won't tell you not to, because it does take a lot of pressure off and removes some of the anxieties you may feel when you start out, BUT there is one major problem with this: A client that doesn't pay is not fully committed (or not committed at all). If you need evidence for this fact, then check the download folder on your laptop and count the number of freebies that you've never looked at. We value things more that we've paid for and we take them more seriously, which in turn means we get better results. So, psychologically speaking, you're doing your clients a favour by charging them.

You should now have a list of two or three ideas for which you've mapped out the deliverables included, the way you want to deliver to or work with your clients and how much you want to charge for each of the ideas.

Validate your idea

In this final step you want to find out whether people would pay for what you want to offer and whether the price you've set (so far) is realistic for your dream client. We're looking at your target audience in more detail in the next chapter, but I wanted to include the validation of the idea here as this is something you'll do every time you develop a new product or service, but you don't necessarily always have to find a new audience.

There are two other angles I want you to look at this from:

1. Is your idea in line with your vision and dream lifestyle?
2. Is your idea in your zone of genius?

I touched on your dream lifestyle when I asked you to

narrow down your list of services above, so you may be happy that it's a fit. If not, go back to the work you did to define your vision and dream lifestyle and reread some of your outputs to make sure you're on the right track.

Secondly, you've spent a lot more time on refining your ideas since you first brainstormed your skills and passions to find your zone of genius, so it's a good time to check in with yourself that you still feel excited about it. You may, very likely, feel a little nervous and scared too - this is a huge step and will likely push you into your stretch zone, and that's a good thing! But it's the kind of anxiety that you feel before a job interview or before you step onto a stage to perform, NOT the kind that you feel when you're in the car with someone that seems to have won their driving licence in the lottery and *really* shouldn't be driving on anything but empty car parks.

To validate that you have designed a service that is in demand, you want to have design conversations with potential customers to discuss ideas and understand whether your offer would help them and how.

This is how you can do this:

- Schedule short calls (15 - 20 minutes - if they are engaged they will speak with you for longer, but you don't want to expect this from the start); or

- Create a survey and share it with your existing audience or people in your network; or
- Utilise the poll function on social media (Facebook groups or Instagram stories, for example).

Design Calls

Start by identifying about five or six people that are in your target market. The easiest way to do this is to post on sites like Facebook or LinkedIn asking for volunteers. This is what I posted not too long ago:

Have you been dreaming of building your own business for years but is stuck in a full-time contract that's paying the bills?

Drop an emoji or message me if you'd be willing to chat with me for 15 minutes.

As a thank you, I'd love to offer you a FREE 30-min coaching call!

I had a number of responses and managed to have all my conversations within a week.

Prepare a handful of questions relating to your ideas that'll help you validate them (and help you focus the conversation), such as:

1. What's their biggest challenge with regards to [the problem you want to help them solve]?
2. How is this impacting their life?
3. Have they hired someone or bought a product to help them solve their problem before? If so, what worked well and what didn't work well for them?
4. What would their life look like if they could [solve the problem you want to help them with]?
5. If they could ask you one question, what would it be?

Now schedule the calls and make sure you take lots of notes and quotes so you have copy for when you get going!

Survey

Alternatively you can create a survey and send out the link to people that you think are a good fit, or ask for volunteers on social media, just like I suggested for the Design Calls above. It's great if you can give them something in return for the favour, because you want to incentivise them, but also start building a memorable relationship with them - especially if they are your ideal client. I have offered them a 30-minute coaching call and have sent them Starbucks gift cards as a thank you. Both were very well received!

There are a number of free tools you can use for the survey. Google Forms (if you use Gmail or the business apps anyway), Survey Monkey or Typeform have all worked well for me. There are some limitations with the free versions, but that shouldn't matter at this stage as you can work around it (some question formats weren't available and you can only create so many forms on the free version). There are some questions that I've used previously:

1. What's your email address? (Add a note explaining why you'd want this, e.g. "I'd like to say thank you and promise to keep it safe.")
2. How young will you be on your next birthday? [Multiple choice with age brackets]
3. How many hours do you work a week and how does this affect your life?
4. How would you describe your work-life-balance?
5. What challenges do you currently face in your life or business, and what effect do they have on your life and business?
6. What did your dream life look like when you first started your business?

7. What is stopping you from living that dream life?

8. If I could wave a magic wand to make it happen, where would you like to be one year from now, who would you be with and what would you be doing?

9. Imagine the perfect transformative coaching program, mastermind, retreat and in-person event has been designed and it's uniquely for you. Thinking: strong focus on actionable strategies, strong mindset and self-belief, a tribe of fierce women who always have your back, personalised coaching, exciting collaborations, lifestyle inspiration and accountability support. What 3 essential elements can you think of that your dream offering needs to have, in order to have you reserve your space in a heartbeat!

You want to tailor these to your offering, of course, but I've had some great responses and again, managed to get lots of copy in my client's language to use in social media posts, on sales pages and in my newsletter, etc. And this means that you can send it to as many people as you like to get a broader view.

Poll on Social Media

Both Facebook and Instagram (in Stories) offer the option to poll your audience. I've found the success of these to be a little hit-and-miss and you can only really ask one question at a time, but these are a great way to engage your audience too, and you will get responses from 'random' people that you wouldn't when doing the design calls or sending out the survey, because they may not be in your immediate network. Here's an example that I used on Facebook:

What's holding you back from starting a side hustle?

- Not sure where to start
- Still researching
- Unsure of how to run it part-time
- Getting distracted too often
- Not enough time

The first option 'Not sure where to start' got the most votes, which gave me a great idea of how I could help my clients. I actually created my free 6-Figure Side Hustle Roadmap following this poll, which is a project plan in Trello that takes you from idea to income step-by-step (you can find the link to it on the page with the bonus material - check the back of the book for all relevant links). People that sign up to it get a link to the board, which they can then create a copy of before working through it for themselves. It's been a great hit, because it solves a problem that many of my clients have.

As mentioned, it would take a number of polls across several days to gather as much information as you can gather in the survey, but it's great to engage your audience and a very easy (and free) tool to use alongside the design calls and surveys.

Your launch product or service

You've gathered a lot of information now and have looked at the options from different angles. You may have one that you feel most excited about, or you managed to validate your short-list and have two or three ideas that are viable.

I'll repeat what I said several pages ago (and am quoting my amazing Mentor, Marisa Corcoran - look her up!): You can absolutely do everything, just not at the same time.

With that in mind, I want you to make a decision right now and not read any further (promise!) until you've decided which offer you want to launch your business with. You can pop it right here where I can see it:

Amazing job! I know that this whole process feels over-whelming at times, but I hope it feels equally exciting. One of the biggest struggles as an entrepreneur, especially once you have this product design process down, is to focus on one idea at a time. There's so much inspiration around us and, once you start working with clients, you get so much feedback that you always have more ideas of how you can serve your audience. Which is why I've already quoted Marisa twice in this book - it's certainly a lesson that I keep having to learn!

The procrastination trap

A word of caution, because this is a critical stage of business journey: you won't find the <u>perfect</u> idea YET. It takes some trial and error, lots of tweaking and experience to get it right. You will have to take the first step at some point and go for it.

"Think of a car driving through the night. The headlights only go a hundred to two hundred feet forward, and you can make it all the way from California to New York driving through the dark because all you have to see is the next two hundred feet. And that's how life tends to unfold before us. If we just trust that the next two hundred feet will unfold after that, and the next two hundred feet will unfold after that, your

life will keep unfolding. And it will eventually get you to the
destination of whatever it is you truly want because you
want it."

JACK CANFIELD IN THE SECRET

Taking action provides clarity. Unless you put yourself and your business out there, you won't get the feedback from the people that you want to buy your services. You can't create a successful business in a black box without external input. As mentioned above, this is such a critical step in your business. So many potential entrepreneurs never move past this point, because they procrastinate forever, while trying to define the perfect product or service. If I can give you one piece of advice that is key for you to be able to make this happen, it's this: DO IT.

The biggest problem we may eventually face when moving too quickly and launching before we feel ready, is that we're going down the wrong path by building a business that may meet a demand in the market and that uses all of our experience, etc. but that we don't feel passionate about or that does not allow us to realise our vision.

I repeatedly work with entrepreneurs who have just broken through to 6-figures and beyond and would reach out to me to get help with setting their business up to scale further. Often we wouldn't even get to talking about scaling, because they admit how they don't actually like, or feel passionate about their work, when I ask them what they love most about their jobs (I ask this to understand what tasks they'd want to outsource and which they'd prefer to do themselves). But here they are looking for ways to do more of something they don't love, because that's what they think they should be doing.

Or they have built a business doing something they enjoy, but that will never allow them to live the life they dream of. I was speaking to a client - a wedding photographer - who wanted to design additional income streams, but wasn't sure where to start. We started where I always start:

"What's your vision?"

Don't worry, I won't share every detail, but there was one dream she shared with me that set my alarm bells ringing: "I want to spend the six weeks of the summer school holidays with my husband's family in South Africa so my daughters can spend more time with that side of the family."

Beautiful image and not even a far-off dream - apart from the fact that she is a wedding photographer and summer is peak wedding season, which she'd miss six weeks of. Trust me, it doesn't matter how passionate she feels about what she's doing, there will be a point where she finds herself taking pictures of a random family on yet another sunny Saturday while not spending time with her girls in the South African sun. This doesn't mean she can never photograph another wedding, but it shouldn't be her core income stream, when it clashes so obviously with a dream of hers.

I've said it before and I say it again: Building and running a business isn't always easy and it takes a certain mindset to do it. But I also know that it's worth it. I wanted to share the examples above to make sure you understand why I recommend the approach outlined in this book. And I also want you to know that you don't have to procrastinate and hold back at this point, while you're waiting for the perfect idea to come to you. As long as you have started by defining your vision and dream lifestyle and therefore know why you're doing this, and have spent some time narrowing down your zone of genius and your idea is smack bang in the middle of it, then you're ahead of so many of your peers.

TARGET MARKET AND DREAM PARTNERS

"There's an audience for everything."

T he approach to finding your target audience is where I differ from most business coaches.

In fact, I had a Facebook ad running for a while with the headline of "Screw Your Ideal Client" and got so many comments telling me that this has several meanings (no, really?) and how inappropriate it was to say that. I didn't mind because all the comments made the ad perform so much better and just proved that my copywriting really did catch people's attention.

Anyhow - of course, I'm not saying that we should forget about our clients. No clients, no sales. But what I am saying is that we should not put them right at the centre of everything we do. We have to put ourselves and our dreams first, or we won't be able to keep building this business when times get tough. Once we know what we want to do and how we want to do it, we can go out and find the people that need what we have to offer. And yes, we may have to make tweaks to our offering so that it's attractive to potential buyers, but it should still be authentically us when we go out there into the world.

Finding your market

Still, one of the first things every business coach in the world will ask you to do as soon as you hire them/buy their course/join their mastermind is to create your ideal client avatar (is it just me that keeps thinking of blue sci-fi figures when they hear the word 'Avatar'?). You give them a name, age, hair and eye colour, a partner, a 7-year-old daughter and a 9-year old son. You define where they live, work, hang out and shop, how much they earn and what books/blogs/magazines they read. You make the assumption that they also binge-watch Tiger King, Love is Blind and Selling Sunset on Netflix while waiting for a Friends reunion.

And then you get into the juicy stuff: Their desires and

dreams on one hand, and their worries and pain points on the other. You assume what it would take for them to finally not wake up at 1:57 am every night. The next step in the process then is to identify a way of how YOU and your business can help them offer a solution for their pain points and a way to make their dreams come true. I doubt I'm the only one that ends up describing themselves, but four years ago, right?

The problem with this approach?

You're building a business based on someone else's needs.

A business that, at times, will take over your life. That you'll put an immense amount of time and energy into. A business that will be your legacy.

All to make *someone else's* life better?

What about your life? Where does this come into your business model?

This is why I flip it on its head and start with your vision and your ideal lifestyle at the core of your business, then ask you to define a product or service that makes you feel excited. And now we're looking at who:

- needs what you have to offer,
- would value what you have to offer,
- you have a connection to in some way, and
- is accessible to you.

However, we'll also look at who you <u>do not</u> want to work with - problem clients that you won't allow in your business (remember when I mentioned boundaries before?).

Start by going back over the notes you took during the design conversations or look at the responses you collected with your survey, if you've completed these already. If not, then go back to the notes you captured as you worked through the idea that you've decided to launch with: What is the problem you solve for your target audience?

_____

_____

Looking at the people you spoke to as you validated your ideas or those that responded to your survey, list out some of the demographics and characteristics you would use to describe them, such as their age, profession or values. Again, if you've not yet had those conversations and you're holding off until you've thought through these next steps on finding your target market, then consider who you think the person is that needs what you have to offer. Think about what data relates to your product and is relevant as they make a decision on whether to work with you or not (i.e. a mother may want to work with another mother when looking for a life coach to make sure she's fully understood, or a professional athlete wants to work with a nutritionist that's a fellow or former athlete etc.).

If you've previously worked with a business coach or completed a course, etc. you may remember more detailed questions, such as who your ideal client may follow online, what books they read, what movies they watch and where they buy their underwear. I've always struggled with these questions and ultimately just put down what was true for me, as I've already mentioned. BUT some of these can be interesting, if they are relevant to the product or service.

For example: I looked at some of the reviews on books that are in my niche to understand what topics were important to my ideal clients and what they were struggling with ("I wish she would have covered off xyz in more detail."). It also means that I know who they follow and can look at their content to get ideas for my own content strategy - without copying them, of course.

Use the space below to list out relevant demographics and characteristics:

_____

_____

_____

_____

Now define some of the target markets that you'd consider working with, such as graphic design freelancers

in retail or women in leadership positions in male domi-
nated industries. It may be that there are two, depending
on the income streams you have in mind, so keep an open
mind for now.

_____

_____

_____

Ask yourself the following questions for each of the
possible target market options you've come up with and
have listed above:

1. Can they afford to pay you for your services or
   product?
2. Can you reach them?
3. Do you have a connection to them to build on
   and leverage?

At the end of this exercise, you want to be in a position
to commit to one target market that you feel excited to be
working with. Remember that you won't find perfect, and
that you may tweak it further as you get to work with your
first clients, have conversations with leads and/or design
calls. It's very likely that you'll niche down further as you
progress, because you figure out that you can offer the

most value to a very specific set of your audience. It's important to put yourself out there and start.

Going global

Something that we've not yet considered and which has more relevance for side hustles than the traditional full-time business is geography. Why? Because time zones are a gift! While we may have often cursed the jet lag we're experiencing back home in London after a week in Los Angeles, the different time zones are amazing for side hustlers. When I first started out, I specifically networked and tried to attract clients in the United States. I was based in the UK already at that time and working with clients in the US meant that I could speak to them in the evening, after I'd finished my day job while it was still their normal working day so I wasn't inconveniencing them by asking to speak to them 'out-of-hours'. The same goes for mornings, especially when you work remotely (full-time or a couple of days a week): If you're happy to get up an hour earlier and can take a call before you start your 9 - 5, with someone that's an hour or two ahead of you, then that works just as well.

This is a great way to get started without it having to impact your performance and availability during your working day. And no, you don't want to have to work evenings forever and you shouldn't, but when building a side hustle, this is often the case for a while.

So, based on your location, make a list of geographies that you'd be able to serve first thing in the morning or in the evening, while it's working hours for them.

_____

_____

By the way, don't worry about the implications of tax, currencies, etc. yet. So many businesses (including mine) operate on a global stage, I can promise you there's ways to deal with that.

Boundaries

Lastly, and I already mentioned this above, I want you to also get really clear about who you DON'T want to work with. To be honest, this is a lesson I had to learn the hard way and most of us do, but being clear on this now means you can tailor your copy and design your sales or onboarding process to weed out the kind of people you can't help.

For example, there's probably no one here that wants to work with people that have bad money habits (unless you're a financial planner) because we all want to get paid, right? But there are other qualities that I don't allow in my business: I already introduced you to my no excuses policy, which means that I don't want clients that always come up with excuses or blame everyone and the world around them for not doing something.

I make this clear in my intake questionnaire, but also mention this when I outline my ways of working during a discovery call because it means that I can always remind them of this later on, if nothing else. Of course, this doesn't mean we never get it wrong and only ever work with our dream clients and superstars, but it will make you approach clients more consciously.

List out some of the qualities you do not allow in your business below:

_____

_____

Building and Nurturing your audience

It's time to come up with a plan of how to best connect with your dream client, so you can start building your audience. At this stage, we want to paint a picture and collect data, so that you can implement later (this is all covered in the third section of the book called 'Implementation'... I know, I'm very subtle and love a hidden meaning).

There are a huge number of ways for you to attract,

build and nurture your audience and it doesn't matter what anyone tells you, there's not one way that works better than all the others. Because it's down to you, your preferences, the way you work and what you feel comfortable doing. I'm not going to tell you that you MUST START A YOUTUBE CHANNEL if you freeze every time you have to get on camera. You're not going to be successful in attracting an audience doing this, because you'd never put any content out. Just like I'm not going to tell you to email your audience at least twice a week, if you hate writing. By default, we won't do something we hate (remember when I told you my take on strengths and weaknesses?).

What I am going to ask you is to push outside your comfort zone and that's different. If you like writing and do it consistently, but you never share your thoughts with the world, then I'm going to suggest you do. If you have animated conversations with your best friend, putting the world to rights, then I will suggest that you consider creating a podcast and sharing some of your advice and wisdom with those that need it. Yes, that is pushing out of your comfort zone, but doing something that you enjoy doing. To get started, think about how you want to create and share content.

Next up are the channels. There are endless possibilities out there these days when it comes to social media platforms and marketing channels, and it can often feel as though we should be *everywhere* to not miss any opportunities.

WRONG.

You want to choose your marketing channels based on your preferences and on those of your clients. I would give even more weight to your preferences, for the very same reasons I gave you above when it comes to your preferred way of showing up for and interacting with your audience: If you don't like a certain social media platform, for example, you won't use it. For me this is Twitter. I have a profile on there, I've tried to tweet away and retweet content in my niche, but at the end of the day, it always fizzled out. So make sure you're happy using the platforms and channels and then check how you can leverage it to reach your audience and nurture them.

First off, decide on two Social Media platforms you want to show up on from the following list:

- Facebook
- Twitter
- Instagram
- Pinterest
- LinkedIn
- Clubhouse

Of course, if you've decided to focus on video when producing your pillar content, then you'll likely use a platform such a YouTube to host this on, but you'll still want to share updates and new contents with your audience through other channels.

Top Tip: Pillar content, by the way, is the content in which you share your expertise and establish yourself as a thought leader. It's also the one piece of content that feeds into all your other posts and emails, etc. If you can create one piece of pillar content (that you put thought and time into) and repurpose the messages from this across your channels, you're winning at the content game! Repurposing is so important when time is precious!

Now that you've identified where you want to show up and how, think about how those channels could work best for your target market. If you're trying to reach overwhelmed managers close to burn-out, then a Facebook Group isn't necessarily the best option, because keeping up with posts would just add to their feeling of overwhelm. Instead, they may prefer something they can listen to on their commute.

Make a list of ways to connect with your audience on your platforms of choice that you feel could work for both you and them. Remember that it doesn't always have to be a teaching or other carefully curated content, but that you can also ask them for input and have fun with them. Show them who you are and how you're the right person for them. Show them your sense of humour and how you love to watch 'My 600lbs Life', because you're a sucker for people turning their life around. By being authentic and sharing a little bit about yourself (and we all have different levels of what we're comfortable with which is ok), you will attract the kind of clients you want to work with.

One last tip, because I've mentioned content and copy quite a lot here. I want you to always consider what your potential clients think they need versus what you know they need. There is a huge difference here. For example, when I have a headache I used to think I needed to take a couple of Paracetamol. When what I really needed was to drink a litre of water and go on a 30-minute walk in the fresh air. I'm mentioning this here, because it's important when it comes to your messaging and to connecting with your audience. Listen out for this when you're having design calls or research interviews with them.

Finding your partners

"If you want to go fast, go alone. If you want to go far, go together."

AFRICAN PROVERB

Now that you know what you want your day-to-day look like, what you want to offer in your business and who you want to work with, it's time to look at who you need to deliver your proposition.

For one, this could be distributors, shops or wholesalers that you want to partner with to sell your products, or a drop-shipping company that can help you fulfil your orders. Or you may want to cooperate with other entrepreneurs to offer services that your clients need, but that you can't (or don't want to) offer - if you're a photographer you could, for example, partner with a brand designer, so your clients are clear on their branding before your shoot.

Why is this part of my business model approach? Because when our resources (both time and energy) are limited, we need to protect them as best as we can and focus on the revenue-generating activities. I can promise you now that you won't be able to run a successful business on a part-time basis without any help. Or maybe you can, but it would be really hard work (and miserable) and you already have that in your corporate role, so let's avoid that!

There are always things that aren't in our zone of genius; tasks that take up too much of our time and energy - time and energy we should be spending adding value. However, making you build a team that you may not want is not the purpose of this exercise. This looks at the options available to enable you to run a business as successfully and with as much fun as possible. That may mean building a big team or it may mean hiring a VA and an accountant. At this early stage, you may want to hire a coach to help guide you or you may want to try and find a mentor instead. It doesn't matter what it looks like, but please know that you DO NOT have to, and shouldn't, do this on your own.

Figuring out what it takes

Start with a big brain dump. Free up 30 minutes of your time and write down all the things you do, want to do, should do or will have to do in your business to build and nurture your audience, stay compliant (think taxes) and to deliver your service or create your product.

Think about:

- Ongoing tasks, such as the accounting or social media management;
- Ad-hoc activities, such as creating your quarterly content plan or writing a proposal for a client; and
- Projects, such as creating a new lead magnet, or launching a new product or service.

List everything out that you can think of and, as you're capturing these, add an 'O' for ongoing tasks, an 'A' for ad-hoc tasks and a 'P' for projects in a second column next to them. You can do this in an Excel spreadsheet, on a piece of paper or on the wall with post-it notes (my favourite - because you can then group things together later).

Note: You'll need four columns to complete the exercises in this chapter, so don't go too mad should you use pen and paper!

As I mentioned earlier in the book too, 30 minutes won't be enough, but you have to start somewhere and I don't want you to put this off because you really need a day or two to capture it all (which we may well do). Just get into the habit of capturing additional tasks in the notes app on your phone or on the back on an envelope that you carry around with you (for a bit of a retro vibe) and then add it to your list when you're back at your desk.

Then, in the third column, add how you feel about the task or project in line with the following:

Add a number between

1 = 'I hate doing this' for tasks or 'this is way out of my comfort zone' for projects

and

5 = 'This is what I get up for in the morning'.

I definitely would encourage you to push outside of your comfort zone and financially, we often have to wear several hats when we first start off, because we can't afford to hire a team or outsource work and there's a lot of activity that we're not necessarily familiar or comfortable with. BUT as soon as you are able to, you want to start picking your battles. Is an hour of your time better spent on a sales call with a potential new client, or even serving a new client, or watching five videos on YouTube to figure out how to add a specific plug-in to your WordPress website? You want to focus your energy on tasks that make a real difference to your business and get experts in to help you with the rest (unless web development is a skill you've been wanting to learn forever…).

At the other end of the spectrum you'll have tasks and activities that you enjoy and are the very reason why you want to start your business - to do more of this and less of the things your boss should really do himself. You want to make sure that you do some of those tasks every single (work) day.

As you can guess, this list will give you a clear idea of what to get help with first! You can then work your way from one to five until you fill your day with only work that lights you up. And yes, I do know that life is not all sunshine and butterflies. As business owners, we can't outsource or delegate all the work that we may not like. We have to take responsibility for some things that we don't enjoy (think taxes… again) and we have to make all the tough decisions, but at a minimum we don't want to feel bored day in and day out, and we want to avoid over-whelm and burn out.

Choosing the players for your team

Starting with the 1's and then working your way up to the 3's (I'll leave you to decide whether you want to outsource or get support with the 4's and 5's), add potential roles to the tasks to get a better understanding of who you need on your team.

Here are some ideas of people that could support you - however, this list is not exhaustive:

- Virtual Assistant
- Copywriter
- Social Media Manager
- Graphic Designer
- Distributor
- Drop-Shipping-Provider
- Accountant
- Solicitor

The above are common support roles for the ongoing and ad-hoc tasks, while the below ideas are more relevant for project-based work.

- Consultants
- Brand Designer
- Website or App Developer
- Coach

- Photographer
- ....

As I said already, you most likely aren't in a position to hire all of the roles at this time, but as your business grows, you'll be able to delegate more and more. It's important to keep this at the back of your mind and to always consider whether you can bundle up a piece of work so that you could hand it to someone else, if you think that there is a return on the investment. This is also one of the big advantages of starting a side hustle, because (depending on your income - I appreciate this doesn't apply to everyone) you may be able to use some of your salary to invest in your business.

Again, always do the maths: as you start serving your clients, you always have to consider which is a better use of your time. If, for example, you can spend an hour coaching a client and you get paid $100 for that hour while a VA would charge you $40 for an hour's work, then you should start to delegate - even more so if time is limited.

As far as projects are concerned, you want to work with consultants or coaches for three reasons:

1. You know your weak spots and need someone to hold you accountable, help you break the

deliverable down into actionable steps and help you find solutions when you get stuck; or

2. You know what you want to do has been done before and you don't want to have to reinvent wheel, so you want someone else to guide you through the process; or

3. You need someone objective to be your sounding board. Someone that is happy to challenge and push you out of your comfort zone, knowing what's possible.

Take it one step at a time, but focus on delegating or getting help with the 1's as soon as you can as they will cost you too much time and will zap your energy!

ACTION PLAN

Y̲ou're at the end of the second section of the book and by now you should now know

- your Zone of Genius;
- how that translates into a viable business proposition; and
- who you want to work with.

Because I'm a sucker for ticking things off a list, I'm including a list of actions you should complete at the end of each section:

1. List out your transferable skills and all the things you feel passionate about.

2. Model out business ideas by combining your skills and passion.
3. Outline your proposition.
4. Design possible income streams and validate them.
5. Define your target market and how you can reach them.
6. Identify partners needed to deliver your proposition.

In the next section, we're going to build a plan to make sure you land your first offer successfully and set yourself up to run your business on a part-time basis. Roll up your sleeves, it's time to take action!

3

IMPLEMENTATION

F inally! It's time to get your hands dirty and write your success story. You've worked through all of the theory and know why you're going on this journey, what you want to do and who you want to serve. Now, we're going to get practical and look at the how - getting you ready to launch!

We'll be looking at some practical ways to prepare to make this business a success and things you need to consider and learn as a business owner. Then we'll dive into mapping out your plan of action, next steps, and how to implement these effectively. And finally, we'll go into more detail of how to set up your back office so that it is possible for you to run this and scale it to six figures on a part-time basis.

By the end of this section you'll be ready to launch

your business (or at least have a clear plan of how to get to the point of launching) and have a clear idea of how to systemise it ready to grow it to a place where it replaces your full-time income.

Ready?

Roll up your sleeves and get stuck in!

SETTING YOURSELF UP FOR SUCCESS

"Opportunities don't happen. You create them."

CHRIS GROSSER

Side hustling isn't for the faint-hearted. I'm speaking from experience when I'm telling you that it'll often feel frustrating as you're trying to juggle all the balls: the balls that aren't necessarily yours but that pay the bills and the balls that are ours and take all of our creative thinking and energy. While it can be exhausting, it's also worth it and such a great strategy: Spending yet another day making money for someone else, using up most of your energy on putting out fires that you're not really interested in - it also gives you the time and money to work on your idea and get the support you need.

So many people that start a business that HAS TO pay the bills (because there isn't another income) often get to a place where they accept any type of work that comes their way. They have to bring money in, right? Before they know it, they are working with a bunch of clients that aren't a good fit, doing work that they're not really interested in and struggling to get off that hamster wheel and make the time to set the right wheels in motion. While you may be desperate to leave your 9 - 5, it also becomes a lot more bearable when you have your exit strategy mapped out and are working on implementing it consistently. So, appreciate the fact that you can take your time to refine your proposition, trial and tweak your services and products and without constantly worrying about how you're going to pay your mortgage next month.

BUT it's also important not to hold on to that security blanket forever. As much as we hate the situation we're in, a regular paycheck is a surprisingly effective bandaid holding things together. The exact reason I just mentioned as an advantage is also a risk because we probably take more time than we need when there isn't a deadline looming or a pressure that forces us to act. This is another reason I start with your vision. You want that picture front and centre of your mind, so that the status quo almost becomes unbearable. So, should you realise that you're holding on to your job longer than is necessary, then set yourself a target date of when you want to leave the corporate world behind, come up with a plan and make it happen. And that's exactly what this third and last section of the book is all about: planning and implementing.

Risk Management

First off, while it's fresh in your mind, I want you to revisit your business model to make sure it's in line with your risk appetite. What do I mean by that?

Some ideas will require you to go all in to be able to launch (if you're considering opening a brick-and-mortar store or co-working venue for example), while others allow you to soft launch and take on some work before you have to go full-time. I shared an example with you of how I started off mostly coaching clients in the US as the time difference meant I could speak to them in the evenings after work. I did more of this again after I had my daughter, because I had childcare when my partner was home. Another alternative is to create and sell mostly (semi-)passive products, which you can create any time of day or night and you can automate or outsource most of the customer service.

Risk management is not often mentioned by coaches

as it's not particularly sexy, but it's as much a part of business as making money is. It's a given. Whenever you go out and try something new, there is a chance that it may not work out or may not work out the way you hoped or as quickly as you thought (which is another GREAT reason to side hustle first, you smart cookie). Accept it and then manage it. And I promise: what may feel like an overwhelming concept is actually pretty simple.

Run a business risk assessment and face up to the potential challenges. It may feel warm and cosy, but burying your head in the sand never did anyone any favours. Allocate some time to thinking through various scenarios and the actions you could take to alleviate them. I use a three-pronged approach: identify, assess and manage.

You start off by pinpointing precisely what the risk is. You then consider how big of an impact that risk stands to make on your business and how comfortable you are with it. Finally, you figure out how to control that damage. It can be an uncomfortable task, but the end result is a stronger, more resilient business and less 2:50am wake up calls driven by panic and uncertainty. When you think of business risk types, a global pandemic probably isn't the first thing that springs to mind, so don't think you have to cover *all* the bases. Hint: it's impossible. But you want to go into this new venture of yours with your eyes wide open and you don't want to do something that causes you anxiety (the uncomfortable kind). Coming back to risk management not being sexy though: Spending serious time thinking through possible business risks, and then factoring in potential actions to minimise the impact of those issues will not only protect you, but also free up crucial headspace that is usually blocked with fear and worry. It will ultimately save you time. It will boost your creative flow. And then you can get back to doing what you do best; running your epic business like the icon you are - now that *really* is sexy.

Outsourcing and Delegating

As you're working through the next chapters, you'll come up with a lot of actions that will need to be done. We already touched on that in the last chapter when we discussed who you will need on your team and in your corner to deliver the business proposition you dream of. Always delegate work outside of your zone of genius as soon as you can - trying to figure things out can take far too long and take up too much energy. Make the most of having some funds from your employment (if that is the case) and invest it in help. The fastest route to success is to focus on what you do best and let others do what they do best. And this does not just apply to our business, but you may be able to use this strategy in your day job too, because there aren't ever enough hours in the day to do everything we need to do, never mind all we WANT to do. We can all agree on that, right?

Hiring a Coach

I know what you're thinking… I would say this, right? But hear me out. Get a coach to help you focus and to hold you accountable - while it's great to not have the pressure of your business having to pay your bills, this can also mean you take a lot more time than needed, so make sure you have someone that helps you focus (to cut down on time figuring it out) and to hold you accountable.

We often turn to friends and family to do this, but they are rubbish at holding us accountable and I can't blame them. When you tell your partner that you "really should finish writing that email welcome sequence" when you really would rather finish watching Game of Thrones, then of course they'll tell you that it's ok to rest sometimes. They'd much rather have you sit next to them than at your desk in another room. And they're right. But it's about balance and short-term pain, long-term gain and we can't have everything. Friends are the same. They often feel threatened when we decide to ditch all those excuses and go for it. It's scary, because they are confronted with making that choice themselves - subconsciously. We don't ask them to, clearly, but it's just a human reaction to compare ourselves and possibly feel as though we should be doing the same (whether that's in line with our long-term goals or not).

A coach, on the other hand, is a neutral party who is focused on the goals you mutually agree on at the beginning of your working relationship. They help you figure out that important next step when you struggle to see the wood for the trees. It's impossible not to get too involved in your own business at times, because you're the expert, you're the one making all the key decisions, you're in the detail all day, every day. Of course it can feel overwhelming when the opportunities are limitless and you have to decide what you're going to focus on first and what step you can take tomorrow to move closer to your goal.

It's also known that working with a coach will accelerate your success significantly if you hire one that has done what you're planning to do. If you've got a new venture on the cards, but you can't pull yourself out of that research phase then this is a great way to stop the vicious cycle of planning and strategising (aka procrastinating) forever. A coach that is specialising in a certain area of business can hold your hand through the process to make sure you can focus on taking action and producing outcomes. However, because I know that finding and hiring a coach that is a good fit for you isn't a quick fix, I've also included some tips on how not to get stuck in the research and strategy phase of a new venture in the box below.

Lastly, you need someone objective to be your sounding board. Someone that is happy to challenge and push you out of your comfort zone, knowing what's possible. You know that verbalising thoughts creates clarity immediately and having someone help you structure the information in your head into an actionable plan is invaluable.

You know your weaknesses, and it's only the responsible thing to do to ask for help and get a plan in place to move forward and succeed despite them.

How not to get stuck in the research and strategy phase of a new venture

1 - Create an outline for your research.

Research can quickly become a black hole; especially when the internet is involved. Go in with a plan of action… and stick to it!

It's important to create an outline for everything you need or want to know in order to move your idea forward. This should include any of your competitors, as well as systems and courses that could help you, with space to record specific information as you review each option.

By having a clear, concise outline (personally, I'm a big fan of a table!), you can stay on track and ensure your research remains focused and intentional.

2 - Be aware of your self limiting beliefs.

It sucks, but there's a high probability that they will come up.

It's natural. Comparison. Lack of inner trust. Fear. Together, these culminate in an internal dialogue that's determined to stop you from grabbing your goals.

You may not be able to stop them; but you can be aware of them.

She has so much more experience than me…

It's already been done…

Who do I think I am trying to offer this...

So, when you're getting closer and closer to the finish line, remember that these beliefs are not real. And you are far, far bigger than them.

3 - Don't try and predict the future.

… because you will not succeed!

Remember, you can only build a strategy and make decisions based on what you know right now, in this very moment. Weighing yourself down in every possible scenario is not only a MAJOR waste of time, but it's also a serious drain on your energy.

Be sensible, but don't tell yourself that you need to have answers to questions that haven't even come up yet. Your strategy can evolve and adapt as you do. There's no reason to have it signed, sealed and delivered from the word 'go'.

Keep it responsive. Focus on the here and now.

4 - Be realistic about your strategy.

You'd be hard pressed to find an entrepreneur who hadn't - at one point - found themselves wonderfully carried away with a new idea.

(Hands up - I've totally been there).

But, if you want to move out of the research and strategy zone and into actual implementation, it's crucial that you keep things practical. Start off by creating a list of what needs to happen for you to get from where you are currently until launch.

Be realistic about it - there's no point in setting yourself obscene goals, only to be disappointed and disheartened when you don't tick them all off of your list.

You need a timeframe that won't set you up for failure; and if this includes bringing someone else on board to help, then factor that in. It's all about pinpointing what or who can help to make your new venture a roaring success.

5 - Ease your overwhelm.

When you've got a million and one things to do, overwhelm can come a'creeping.

My way to keep overwhelm at bay? I only ever focus on the next step.

Sure, I'll always have a long-term plan buzzing away in the background, but when it comes to my day-to-day work, I always ask myself "what is the next thing I can do?"

This stops you from getting bogged down in the steps that you don't even need to consider yet. As a result, it's far easier to step out of the planning phase and start bringing your idea to life.

Use your time wisely

I mentioned this already at the beginning of the book when I wanted you to free up some time in your day-to-day for your business, but want to mention some tips on saving time again in this context. We all like a little gossip, but you'll need your lunch breaks and you'll want to finish on time, so be aware of how you spend your day. Also, while sitting on public transport isn't glamorous, you can get more done on a train than in a car, so look at different commuting options depending on your circumstances. There are a lot of ways we can save a little time every day:

The easiest way and quickest way to free up time is to say no. You can do it in a direct (German) manner, or more graciously. Try "Thanks for thinking of/trusting me, but other commitments mean that I'm not able to help you (this time)." The other commitments include those you make to yourself, your family, your business, your goals or dreams. And no, you don't have to go into more detail. If this in a professional setting, then feel free to recommend someone else that may be able to help instead.

Then try to cut out negative energy. Admittedly this one is easier said than done, but also has an immediate effect. Cut down contact with people that get you down. Unfortunately, most of us are emotional sponges and being surrounded by negative energy leads to more procrastination, more doubting, more delaying and scenario planning, more time doing everything but taking steps forward.

Schedule repeat appointments for admin tasks. Make a list of all the admin tasks you do regularly or SHOULD DO regularly and decide how often you'd ideally do them so it's not annoying, but also doesn't take up your whole day. Then add a repeat appointment into your diary to make sure you have the time and the reminder to get on with it. To give you ideas, for me, this is: my expenses (weekly), unsubscribing from irritating emails (monthly), checking my finances (monthly), ordering repeat prescriptions and my dogs worming tablet (quarterly) and making dentist appointments (every six months).

Similar to 'saying no' above, you can also stop doing or do less of things. Think through all the things you are doing and find at least two that you can stop doing or do less of. Did you volunteer to manage the Instagram account for your networking group and it takes you at least a couple of hours a week now to prepare and schedule the posts? Is it always you that takes the boys to football practice and picks them up again? Maybe it's time to be honest and say that you currently struggle to keep up and that you'll have to take a break from doing what you're doing, or you want to rotate, so you only have to do it every three weeks or so. Some other ideas:

- Stop hitting snooze in the morning;
- go on social media for only two 30-minute periods a day, not every chance you get (turn off notifications so your screen doesn't light up every two minutes); or
- reduce the number of trips to the kitchen during which you also wash up, empty the dishwasher and water the plants, by making a thermos of coffee or tea first thing in the morning.

Adapt your life to make it as effortless as possible. Of

course, you can do the obvious and get a cleaner (and if you can afford it, then absolutely do it), but it can be simple adjustments, such as a meal planning, ordering your food shop online and having it delivered and keeping your shopping list digital, with a section of 'favourites'. This is a great area to standardise: remove decisions by having the same breakfast and some of the same dinners, but add in a couple of new ones each week, for example. Brainstorm other things that you could simplify and speed up.

Another tip on time management: By scheduling short sprints of focus (e.g. 25 minutes), you don't feel as though you have to force yourself not to look at your phone for hours and it creates a fake deadline - especially useful for those of us that thrive under pressure. The short period not only encourages a single task focus, but also allows you to schedule two, three or four sprints with quick 5-minute-Instagram-and-toilet-breaks in between for tasks that take longer. I would encourage you to take a longer break after four sprints though and even to get some fresh air, if possible. 25 minutes is very manageable, but see what works for you. You may be able to stretch to 40 minutes or maybe want to start with just 20 minutes. There is no right or wrong as long as you fully focus on the task in front of you during that time period.

Work on your mindset consistently

Building a business is tough (full-time and part-time) so make sure you're prepared. As already covered at the beginning of the book, you'll always have doubts and limiting beliefs to deal with and you will feel fear. Unfortunately, working on your mindset is a lot like losing weight: there's no magic pill or a switch that you can flip. It takes work, consistently making the right choices and constant reminders to be able for you to succeed.

One of my favourite ways to remind myself to work on my mindset is by surrounding myself with inspiration. This could be people or things; whatever works, make sure you are surrounded by nuggets of wisdom and inspiration that keep you motivated. Quotes, pictures, t-shirts, mugs and even tattoos are fantastic ways to regularly remind yourself why you are on this journey. They're the daily signs needed to keep you on the right track and excited about that final destination. I know it's not everyone's cup of tea (such a British thing say!), but I have a mug with a crown on it and another one that says "Good Vibes Only". I have a print in a frame behind my desk that says "Meet me in New York" because that's where I'll have an office one day. AND I took it a step further and got a tattoo on my foot that's a very personal reminder for me to stay strong when times are rough.

I'm going to dive into more detail on the fear here

because it's such a central and important aspect of business. Going out on your own means that you'll consistently push outside of your comfort zone (everything else would be boring, right?), which means you'll also have to deal with your own resistance. Fear as a business owner is a rite of passage when you are scaling your empire. Turning that fear into fuel? That's the real sweet spot. We are taught fear from a young age. We're scared of the bogeyman in our closet, the monster under the bed. We either adore the adrenaline of a play park or back away from it at all costs. When we fall and scuff our knees, we start to understand risk (not that it stops us tripping over and over and over again). If our parents shout at us, we cry. The "F" word is a biggie… one that seamlessly evolves and moves into adulthood. But those fears? They change. Suddenly we aren't scared of ghost stories anymore; instead we fear failure, rejection, public speaking. The list is endless.

What if I told you that fear was a *good* thing? That it was all about how we used it? I believe that fear can be a valuable way to boost your business. It can present us with an abundance of opportunities… if we learn how to control it. It's something I've really dug deep into as I've grown my business. Because honestly? Fear held me back for a long time. It was fully, undeniably and painfully in the driver's seat: both for my business and my life. It took a long time to change that. But the moment I learned how to harness fear and turn it into something positive, my entire outlook changed. And I want to help you experience that too.

For one, fear means something big is going to happen. Way, way, WAY back, big equalled bad. We strived to stay small - it was safe. Now we know that big can mean an amazing opportunity. The problem is, our brain struggles to process that; it pops 'danger' and a 'big opportunity' in the same category. This results in anxiety, nerves, and a tendency to avoid the *thing* altogether. But remember: while your mind might be struggling to process this as a good thing, your heart will know. So trust it. Take the energy pulsing through your nervous system and use it to propel you forward.

Then, build your fear muscle. You cannot pass through life without disappointments and some 'failures'. You know the ones I mean; the pitch we didn't win... the subscribers falling off of your mailing list... the lead that says 'no'... the article HuffPost refused to publish. Also, fear can push us further. It can be a huge motivator to break out of the box and push forward, full steam ahead. Think about it; when you have a strong vision, it makes your comfort zone (or current scenario) feel less and less attractive. Actually, it can feel damn awful. Which means we become fearful of remaining stuck in that position. The idea of it can be terrifying. And so we need to move; we use that fear to wave goodbye to where we are so that we can dive straight into where we want to be. At the time, it sucks. Well and truly. However, my anxiety has taught me that those disappointments are easier to deal with the more often I face them. It's the only way to overcome fear. Picture it as a special muscle - the more practice it gets, the stronger it becomes.

Fear has the ability to protect us because when we get too comfortable, we make mistakes. And while mistakes can help us grow, they can also be a bit of a pain. It allows us to better organise and prepare ourselves - this, as a result, can eradicate some of those mistakes. I'm not advocating for "always waiting until you're ready"; spoiler alert, we rarely will ever feel *ready*. What I am saying is that a healthy dose of fear means we are more likely to pay attention to instructions, checklists, and guides before throwing ourselves headfirst into something we aren't prepared for.

Lastly, fear can help you learn more about your clients. For those who work directly with clients (for example, coaches) or employees, we can use the concept of fear to find out more about how they are personally feeling. You could be asking them to push out of their comfort zone or take on a new role... ask them, how does that make them feel? This can help you better build your service around them and deliver the best possible experience and solution to their needs. Plus - it makes for brilliant content! Share their thoughts and fears... be relatable! This will show that you really understand your clients' emotions and are well equipped to support them.

Definitely don't ever let fear hold you back. Instead, use it as an indication that you and your business are growing... that huge things are coming!

Lastly and, arguably, most importantly, it takes a shift in mindset and the belief that you WILL do it. And people around you that will hold you accountable and inspire you to keep pushing - and this is what I'm here for!

Focus on your path

A side hustle, more than any other business set up, requires you to focus.

For one, it's super important not to compare yourself to other entrepreneurs in the same space, because you can't win. It'll always feel like they get more done and it'll get you down. It's difficult, because I'd always encourage you to surround yourself with peers that are on the same or a similar journey as they'll help so much on those days when you're struggling. They believe in you when you can't and they celebrate your wins with you. BUT you have to remember that everyone's circumstances are completely different: their personal situation such as how much time their partner can spend looking after the kids, their day job and how demanding it is (if they have one), how much they have to learn about building a business compared to you, their financial situation which impacts the support they can get or even how they process information and develop ideas. These are just a load of examples, of course, but I wanted to make sure that you understand that comparison doesn't add any value whatsoever.

This is a huge problem with social media and the online business space too. We are getting so much information on a daily basis; information that's carefully curated or not (more on this in a minute). It's such a fine line between inspiration and frustration, so make sure you're conscious about the way you interact and absorb information. And I'm not just talking about people who are shouting about how they just won their third new client this week paying them a juicy 5-figure sum to work with them (and they'd love to teach you how to do the same), or those that grew their Facebook group by 200 members overnight with one post.

I'm also talking about the sheer volume of information out there and so easily accessible to us now. While it can be a blessing, it can also be a huge challenge. There's always something else we could or should try:

- Advice from a different coach that makes complete sense when he talks about it on that podcast you're listening to.

- Another social media platform that works a treat for your friend.
- That quiz that you have to build as it's the one thing you MUST do to grow your email list.
- And so on and so on.

It's exciting for a while and then it gets so exhausting. And it often takes us a little while of doing it ALL before it sinks in that we don't actually enjoy most of it and, even if it worked like magic, we still wouldn't want to keep doing it long-term!

I'm sure you think I sound like a broken record player when I tell you how to avoid shiny-object-syndrome and make decisions based on your vision, dream lifestyle and zone of genius. When you see something new that you're not currently doing, or haven't tried yet, and you wonder whether it is an opportunity, then make sure it gets you closer to your vision, is doable when living your dream life-style (yes, a daily live video at 8 am every day is effective in building an audience, but it also means you can't take your kids to school after having breakfast with them) and is not one of your weaknesses (something that drains you - even if you are easily able to do it). See how important that foundational work we did in the beginning is? We always go back to it to make decisions. If it turns out there is something you want to try, then make sure you don't spend hours or days or months preparing and planning again, but go back up to the box with my tips on how not to get stuck in the research and strategy phase of a new venture.

One clarification though: I'm not telling you to never veer off the path and not go after an exciting opportunity because it's not something you considered before - but make sure it's worth it! Have huge amounts of fun doing something crazy, something to tell your grandchildren about one day.

Prioritise like your life depends on it

Because your dream life actually does. Depend on it, I mean. Your inbox has 2783 unread emails, your calendar looks like lunch - or peeing for that matter - is not a thing anymore and your team has to collectively jump on you and wrestle you to the ground to get enough time with you to ask a question. It feels overwhelming and unproductive, so the below quote really resonated when I heard it the other day:

"Make sure the urgent doesn't overwhelm the important."

I had only recently started listening to Podcasts, mostly to distract myself from road rage as my commute has increased significantly after moving to the South Coast. I thought I'd start with one of the best: the Tim Ferriss Show. He interviewed Eric Schmidt, Former Google Executive Chairman & CEO, the first time I listened and it was good. Like really good. Unexpectedly, I had to get to grips with a previously unknown side effect of podcast listening: having to pull over at the side of the road to take notes. Twice. Trust me to make something that is meant to make the journey go by quicker, make the journey take longer. My parents must be so proud... "Make sure the urgent doesn't overwhelm the important" was one of the quotes I jotted down in my notebook somewhere off the A31 in Hampshire.

When organising workload, we need to understand whether a task is urgent, important or both to define a next step in dealing with a task.

- **Important tasks** are usually linked to achieving a goal we have set ourselves or an outcome we want to or should deliver. While they are important, they are not always urgent and easy to push down the list of to do's.
- **Urgent tasks** can often be linked to other people's goals or deliverables, but definitely have a tight deadline or are on the critical path to delivering an outcome. This could be at your day job or even friends and family asking you for help.

Neither of the above explanations are set in stone, of course, but are for guidance. Trust your instincts.

If you categorise them using important and urgent as criteria, you'll quickly be able to decide what to do. A task that is both important and urgent should be completed straight away. Something that's urgent, but not important could, for example, be done by someone else. Make sure you schedule time for anything that's important but not urgent and don't touch anything that's neither important nor urgent - you don't have time for that sort of thing (anymore).

Rubber and glass balls

I came across this prioritisation technique by coincidence when I was trying to arrange a meeting with a client when she said: "I'd love to, but can't do that afternoon, because I'm throwing a party for my nanny who's leaving after seven years with us. It's a glass ball moment. Sorry!"

"A what," I asked, most likely with a slightly scrunched up face.

"A glass ball moment. If I drop that ball I won't get it back."

She went on to explain how rubber balls bounce back. That work project that you had to drop to attend your primary school teachers funeral will still be there tomorrow. However, your son's preschool graduation will never happen again. That's a glass ball moment - if you drop it, that's it.

Huh.

Of course, those examples are pretty obvious and not every decision we have to make is quite that clear. Your priorities depend on your values and aspirations in life and they can shift depending on circumstances.

For example, we'd probably all agree that - generally - family comes first and is glass while work comes second and is rubber. BUT you may get a work-related opportunity that can shape your career and life, which you decide is a glass ball moment. And because your family knows they are glass for you, they understand that you have to put them down - with careful consideration - to make the most of this opportunity.

When deciding priorities, you need to first understand whether something is glass or rubber for you. Ask yourself some or all of the questions below to figure it out:

Is it in alignment with my vision? Go back to your big vision to understand whether something is in alignment with your dreams or not. Quite frankly, if it isn't, then it's not a ball you should be juggling at all. Put it down.

What will it take for me to recover if I dropped this ball? Many things we worry about would still be there tomorrow and it's just about managing expectations. Did you commit to delivering something, but could go back and ask for an extra day without it being a big deal? Is this opportunity likely to come up again?

Does my juggling of this ball impact someone else? Trying to understand who else is affected by your choices and the importance of whatever is going on for them is crucial. Of course, you know that the GCSEs are only one little stepping stone on this journey called life, but you can be damn sure that it's the biggest deal ever to your daughter right now.

Does this ball have a long-term impact on my life? Yes, it feels important right now, but will you still care about this six months from now? We get so caught up in our day-to-day life, focusing on what's right in front of us, wanting to do the best job possible, that we lose sight of the bigger picture. Take a moment and a step back. Will it still matter?

Deciding priorities is tough. Things move quickly and often without our ability to influence them. You learn to trust your intuition of what is the right thing to do, and rightly so. However, it's important to take the time to form your vision, ready to recall and to decide which values are most important to you, and you'll immediately know whether something is a rubber or a glass ball. And if you handle your glass balls carefully and considerately, then it's ok to put them down sometimes.

Get your cheering squad in place

I gotta be honest, the relationship piece of transitioning from employee to CEO was the hardest piece of this big old puzzle to master. The thing is, unless you are a business owner or at least an aspiring business owner, it's difficult to understand why you would take the risks you take, work all those extra hours without getting paid for them (immediately) or give up the dental insurance that you had as a free benefit in your corporate role. You'll realise this quickly when speaking to your friends and colleagues and they don't quite know how to respond to some of your problems. And we can't blame them - they are in a completely different place! It's hard when, all of a sudden, your best friends can't help you anymore with the things that are top of your mind. There are two things that happened for me as I was faced with this (and it can feel quite uncomfortable and scary):

First, I knew I had to go out there and find new friends. People that get me, that are on the same path and that would be able to help me brainstorm solutions. This wasn't as easy as it may seem, as it was a prime opportunity for my impostor syndrome to rear its ugly head. I signed up for a networking meeting and as I walked into the room of business owners I couldn't help but wonder who I thought I was to be in the same room with these 'proper' entrepreneurs! But I persevered, and have been able to build some valuable relationships and supportive friendships. Not only that, but since that first networking meeting, I've also met two people that are now my partners in a business that I co-founded during the pandemic and that's taken off more quickly than any of my other ventures to date.

There are so many opportunities to network - online and offline - and find mentors and friends. This could be memberships run by business coaches, in-person or virtual events and summits, training courses and workshops.

Just like I found myself heading to Florence for a workshop a couple of years ago. On my own! When I first saw this workshop advertised (I came across it by coincidence), I signed up within the hour. A writing workshop in Italy? HELL YES! I was peeing-my-pants-with-excitement excited and couldn't believe my luck! I had never been to Italy before either and am a dedicated lover of all things quintessentially Italian: espresso, prosecco, pasta, pizza, gelato, dark-haired men, sunshine. This was a sure bet. Until the date came closer and closer and I had to actually think of logistics and what to pack. I started to get more and more anxious. I begged my boyfriend to come with me, because I didn't want to go on my own. I suggested to my friend to get a flight and we could share the room. And then in the end, I was on my own as I scanned my boarding pass to go through to security at Heathrow and headed for the plane taking me to Italy. (By the way, I travel alone all the time, but had never before been to Italy or to a workshop where I didn't know a single person…). And - unsurprisingly - I had one of the best weekends of my life! I learned so much and met some of the loveliest people that I now get to call my friends. One of the reasons I was über-excited when I signed up was that the class was taught by one of my idols - a copywriter I had been following for years and whose newsletter I would open AND read EVERY. SINGLE. TIME. (Crazy, right?!) Her name is Laura Belgray. I have never had celebrity crushes (apart from my love for Eminem, which is not a crush, as us being together is fate - completely different), but I follow successful entrepreneurs like my dog follows the trail of fox pee - they inspire me so much and remind me that anything is possible.

Why am I sharing this story here? To show that it's absolutely worth pushing outside of your comfort zone and exploring. I came back from that weekend in Florence and completely changed my business - something that was only possible because I have had the opportunity to brainstorm ideas with people that were telling and showing me that anything is possible.

Secondly (remember how I said there were two things that presented themselves as challenging when starting my own business..), I had to cut off some 'friends'. This sounds harsh and may make you feel uncomfortable, but it wasn't actually that difficult. You'll soon find that starting and running a business (as a side hustle) naturally takes a lot of your time and energy. I've mentioned before how there's always something else you could do, another idea to pursue, a lead magnet to update, a course to create, etc. More so than ever, time is money. Which means you'll be even more careful of how you spend your time and who you spend it with. For me, in some cases this meant that I didn't want to waste time or energy with people that were negative and not supportive of what I was doing. I didn't pick arguments or officially 'break up' with anyone, but it just happened. You'll find that this will happen for you too, now that you're clear on what you want your life to look like and you're setting yourself up to make this a reality. American entrepreneur Jim Rohn famously said that we're the average of the five people we spend the most time with, so we want to make sure those five people are supportive and inspiring.

BUT this doesn't mean that I only have friends that run their own business and refuse to speak to my old friends. I now just make sure they mean enough to me and are excited and happy for me and this journey that I'm on.

Don't get fired from your day job

If you're in employment, then you want to leave on good terms when the time comes, as you never know who your future customers will be! Not just that, but of course you want to avoid having to take your business from side hustle to paying all the bills overnight or so much of your effort would be wasted.

Make sure you allocate enough time and energy to deliver what's expected of you and in the quality that is in line with the quality that you'd deliver in your business. Every single one of your colleagues and stakeholders could be potential customers for you going forward, so make sure they remember you as someone that they'd want to work with again.

Also, you will have days when your job is incredibly demanding and frustrating. On those days, it'll be difficult to move from your job to your side hustle and feel motivated. You'll question whether it's all worth it. Those will also be the days when you feel like you're making *no progress at all* in your business, when you are - just not as quickly as others seem to be. Make sure that you allow yourself to take a break. While it all feels too overwhelming and your instinct is telling you to curl up and binge-watch Love is Blind on Netflix (and I'm not here to blame you), you have worked too hard to just let go. So instead, make a list of the priority activities in your business to keep it ticking over (even if it doesn't make money for you right now). Think of a car that you don't use for months and then when you finally get in it, it won't start because the battery is dead. Your business is not dissimilar, if more complex. (Gentle reminder: Communication -

with your clients, but also your team if you have one - is most important and a minimum requirement!) Go back to basics and block out the minimal amount of time needed to keep things going on a daily basis. Again, when the proverbial hits the fan, the basics are most important. If a Facebook live or a post on Instagram is the only thing you manage to do, then so be it.

My last tip for you to set yourself up for success and make sure you make this happen, even with a day job? Set milestones that force you to launch - commit to dates and make them public, so that you have to stick to them. At some point, you'll have to pull the plaster off and it'll be so worth it!

How to plan and set those milestones is what the next chapter is all about.

CREATE (REALISTIC) PLANS AND TAKE ACTION

"Well done is better than well said."

BENJAMIN FRANKLIN

Remember when I said it takes both mindset and action for success to happen? If you'd only take one piece of advice away from reading this book, I hope it'd be this: Small, consistent steps add up to big things. I always tell my clients to prioritise consistency over intensity. Of course, it's an amazing feeling when you get to spend a whole day focused on something and you can see the output at the end - feeling like the Queen of productivity (you can get in line right behind me). But, and it's really more like a BUT, those all-day sprints rarely happen. Consider them a bonus, but make sure you're set up to take those small steps every day.

Planning out what it'll take

Similar to the big brain dump I suggested when we were trying to figure out what partners you'd need to run your business successfully, I need you to get everything down on paper that you think you need to get done to successfully launch your first offering.

I know I've mentioned this before, but I'm a huge fan of post-it notes because you can take them and rearrange them to group tasks together in similar buckets. Mind-mapping apps are great for this too, however, you can also just get some Flipchart paper (the bigger, the better) and some marker pens and do this the old school way.

Use your customer journey to help you think through this and consider questions such as:

- How will my customer learn about me or find me?
- How do they get in contact or how do I capture their contact details so that I can get in touch with them?
- How can I tell them more about me so that they'll want to buy from or work with me?

- How and when do I sell to them?
- How do they pay me?
- What do I need to have in place to deliver my product or service?
- What support would my clients need once they've bought from me and how do I provide this?

Start by listing all the deliverables you need. The systems you need to have in place, the products you need to design and build, sales pages and email sequences. You can find some examples in the box below.

Your Brand

Decide on your business name

Buy the domain

Design a logo

Create your key message

Your Funnel

Create your lead magnet

Write your welcome sequence

Set up your funnel

Nurture System

Design your system

Set up your channels

Create your schedule

Product Development

Check feasibility

Design your product/service

Build your product/service

Marketing

Map out sales funnel

Create a sales page

Launch

Your launch strategy

The customer journey

Prepare your assets

Go Live

Operations

Define your core tasks

Create templates

Choose tools

Hire partners

Once you have your deliverables mapped out, you want to go into more detail and map out the individual

CREATE (REALISTIC) PLANS AND TAKE ACTION   175

actions required to deliver that specific output. I'll go through some of the above in a bit more detail now, so that you can extract a lot of the actions from that and add it to your mind map or wall of sticky notes.

Your Brand

This is equally the most exciting and the most terrifying part of starting a business: coming up with your brand name. The pressure of trying to think of the next 'Google' or 'Uber' or 'Apple'… Of course, it depends on what your vision is (I'm so predictable, I know), but unless you're planning to go all in, pitch your idea on Dragon's Den or Shark Tank (depending on where in the world you are) and build the best thing since AirBnB, then it's totally ok to use your name. However, it's also fun to get creative and come up with a name that is specific to your service or product and that'll be easier to sell down the line. There are a lot of company name generator pages online (just search for them), but before you know it three days have passed and you can't make a decision because you have too many choices now. Have fun with this, but make sure it doesn't hold you up - it's absolutely fine to use your name for now and change it later. Make sure you check that the domain is available for whichever name you choose and that it's not already trademarked. If the domain is available, then buy it as soon as you can, but don't worry about a website yet.

Putting a website together is a big piece of work and not necessarily needed straight away. You can also just build a landing page using forms and templates by your email management provider or specific landing page service. If you want to pull something together, then go for it, but I don't want you to spend an incredible amount of time and effort on designing and creating something that will most definitely change as you narrow down on your services, improve your messaging and get clearer on the kind of client you want to work with. A website is not absolutely necessary to get started.

However, if you're anything like me, something that will help for sure is a logo. I love giving whatever I'm working on an identity and it's such a great asset to share with the world when you're announcing your launch. Depending on your budget and how important this is to you, you can choose to work with a branding designer, spend $20 on Fiverr or Upwork to get one done or even design one yourself on a website such as Canva. Remember that this is the logo to get you started, not necessarily the final product!

Lastly, create your key message - that one sentence that you can share with the world. It should include who you help, what you help them do and what result(s) this means for them. Alternatively, you can include who you help, what you help them do and an objection, something I did in one of my key messaged: "I help women grow a profitable business their way (without quitting their 9-5 job or other things you've been told you have to do to make it happen)". I added the objection of 'without quitting their 9 - 5…' in because that's something that comes up for my clients when they think of building a business.

To summarise, some of the actions you want to note down for this are as follows:

1. Decide on a company name
2. Buy domain
3. Design logo
4. Set up landing page
5. Draft key message

Your Funnel

Once you have a name and a landing page, you really want to start building that audience. Growing and nurturing your audience is what takes the most effort and most amount of time of any of the activities. Unlike in the traditional brick-and-mortar retail setting, it's very, very rare that a customer stumbles across your website and immediately decides to buy from you. You need to catch their attention first (which is almost the hardest part considering the amount of information and options online) and then allow them to get to know, like and trust you before they're willing to spend their hard-earned cash with you. And because no audience equals no sales, this is your utmost priority.

I'm not going to go into loads and loads of detail of how a funnel works because most of you will be familiar with the concept - if not as a business owner, definitely as a consumer. Every time you enter your email address in exchange for something free, whether that is a download, a quiz result, a discount code, etc., you're entering a funnel. That business now has your contact details and often also the permission to contact you. You'll either get a number of emails in which they tell you more about what they do and how they can help you, you get their weekly or monthly newsletter or further offers. This is exactly what you want to create for your business.

First, you need to create a lead magnet - an asset or offer that you can share with leads for free in exchange for their email address. You'll capture the permission to contact them at the same time (explicitly or implicitly). Try and think of a workbook, a checklist, guide or something similar on a topic that relates to your service and will help a person in your target market. You want to give value, but you also don't want to give too much away for free - look what others in your niche offer for inspiration and then try and think of a way of how you can improve on that.

Once you've decided on the lead magnet you want to create, draft an outline and then write the content. Add some design elements (or your logo as a minimum) or you can outsource the design and, lastly, save the file as a PDF. The easiest and least complicated way to share this with your audience after they sign up is via a link to a location on your drive. Just make sure you change the settings for that file so that anyone on the internet with the link can view the item.

The next thing you'll want to do is write a welcome sequence: A series of emails that will automatically be sent to new subscribers as soon as they sign up. The first email usually contains the link to the free download or video, etc. while the following emails will tell your potential client more about you and what you do. This is the first step towards building that know, like and trust factor that I've mentioned before. Often these emails are scheduled to go out one a day for the next five or six days, but you could also leave a couple of days or so between emails to make them last longer and not bombard your new subscribers. That's completely down to you.

Lastly, with the content and asset ready, it's now time to build the actual funnel, which facilitates the capture of leads. You want to design a landing page (using a template in your email management system), create your email sequence and set up the automation so that everything works without you having to get involved. Test it and switch it live. And just like that you're ready to go!

To summarise, these are some of the actions you need to complete:

1. Create your lead magnet;
2. Write your welcome sequence (at least 5 - 6 emails);
3. Sign up for your email management system of choice;
4. Create your landing page;
5. Set up your email sequence;
6. Set up your automation;
7. Test and switch live.

Nurture System

While growing your audience is important, nurturing

it is even more crucial. You want them to one day not just buy from you, but for them to become your fans - the kind of customer that tells everyone about you. Whether you have launched services yet or not, you can always start sharing your message, deliver teachings or generally interact with those that have chosen to hear from you.

There are lots of different ways to do this, some of which we've looked at before when I asked you to define your target market and think about where you would find them. You could, for example, invite them to a Facebook group (which is great for delivering free training and teachings through Facebook Live videos), you can ask them to follow you on Instagram or use email marketing to share a weekly newsletter with them.

Once you have decided on the channels you want to use, you can set them up using your company name and start posting (if it's social media). Especially if you open a Facebook group to grow your audience, you want to make sure you have a few posts and a little video in there ready before people join so they have something to look at when they do.

Then come up with a plan of what you'd like to post and share with your audience. For ease, you could decide themes for months (e.g. January is all about strategy) and then have topics for each week (e.g. for January these could be topics such as goal setting, promotion planning, prioritisation techniques, etc.), which you can then base your content on. For Facebook groups, you could have set posts for certain days, such as Motivation Monday or Wednesday Wins (you can then create images that you can use every week which cuts down on effort too), etc. I would, however, still post advice and original content at least 2 - 3 times a week. You could do this in a post or as a live video. Do what feels right for you and your audience, but also consider if it's manageable with the limited time you have or if you can outsource (at least some of) it sooner, rather than later. Creating a schedule will help you so much on those days when you're struggling to think creatively.

To summarise, these are the actions you want to complete:

1. Brainstorm your nurture channels and activities;
2. Set up your channels;
3. Create a content schedule;

Product Development

You want to start by choosing the service that you want to launch with first, if you haven't already done so when we were looking at the income streams earlier. Again, consider what would be easiest to sell when you first start. You need, for example, a large audience to sell an online course, because conversion rates are often only between 1% and 3%, but selling one-to-one services can also work with smaller audiences. Also think about how much time you have and how soon you want to launch, or alternatively, how much money you have to spend to get that first offer out there sooner?

Once decided, you want to check feasibility. While you very likely have done that in your design calls already, I want to mention it here in case you come back to this section in the future as you're developing another offer. You want to go into a bit more detail to make sure that a market exists for what you have to offer and that people are willing to buy it. If that's a yes, then consider how big the opportunity is (i.e. how big is your potential target market). Look at the competition and think about how you can set yourself apart, but also whether it's worth it: is the margin big enough for you to make it worth the effort?

If you're certain you want to go ahead, then start designing your product or service. Decide how you want to serve, what's included or what the product looks like (the deliverables) and what the price is going to be (but also whether you may want to offer an instalment plan to make it accessible to a bigger audience).

Lastly, put in place everything you need to deliver your new offering - content, platforms, questionnaires, templates and so on.

Bear in mind that there are whole books and university

courses on product development, so the above is just a snapshot of what's needed, but it includes everything you need to get an offer out there. Feedback from your clients and audience once you launch will be the most valuable tool in developing your service or product further.

To summarise, you want to complete the following actions (if you haven't already) to develop your product or service:

1. Choose your product or service;
2. Check feasibility;
3. Design your product or service;
4. Build your product or service;

Marketing

You already have a big chunk of your (initial) marketing effort in place with your funnel and nurture system, but this part of the process is specifically about launching your first offer.

Because you already have social media pages by now, and an email list set up, you can dive straight into mapping out your sales funnel. You want to design a sales process that works for you and is aligned with the investment to work with you. For example, you want to make sure to have a free discovery call and possibly even an application process for higher investments such as one-to-one coaching over three or six months for two reasons: You want to make sure people are committed, but you also want to make sure they are a fit - i.e. you can help them and want to work with them.

For lower investments, however, you can, and want to, automate as much as possible. In this case you want to set up a payment page and allow them to book time with you through a scheduling system, because the last thing you want to do is spend three hours going back and forth trying to find a convenient time for both of you when they only pay you for one hour.

At this stage, map out what this looks like, then put in place the resources (i.e. create accounts with payment solutions and online scheduling apps) and make sure they integrate so that it's one effortless process for your clients. This will be fronted by a sales page, which you can set up using a template in your email management system, or a specific landing page provider, as I've mentioned previously. The most challenging element of creating a sales page is writing the copy. It's a little like writing a CV, which I consider one of the worst jobs in the world. But also, there's a reason why copywriting is such a big business these days. Make sure you have something that grabs the attention of your ideal client and show them that you 'get them'. You can do this by quoting some of the people you interviewed or surveyed when designing your income streams as this means you're using their language. You can then share with them why you have the solution and what that looks like, so the features of your product or service, and how this helps them. You then want to build trust by telling them why you're the right person to work with and - if you have these - add some testimonials, because social proof is the most convincing argument. Lastly, include a section that tells them how to take action. While you tell them here what the process looks like, and you'll have a button that allows them to complete the application form or buy there and then, you still want to have those calls to action after every section of the sales page that allows them to buy or apply immediately. Once you've written the content and designed the page, make sure you test it and all the links are working, before publishing it. It's always a good idea to get a third party to click through the process too.

And with that... you're ready to sell!

To summarise, these are the actions you need to take to market your product or service:

1. Map out your sales funnel;
2. Create the resources and tools needed;
3. Set up the funnel;
4. Write content for sales page;
5. Design sales page;
6. Test your sales page and funnel;
7. Publish your sales page;

Launch

Your sales page is published, you have a way to take your customer's money and for them to book time to work with you, now you just have to let them know that they can!

There are different ways to launch your business or product and it's up to you to find the way that works best for you. You could do a soft launch, where you put your service or product out there to buy and then share it with as many people as possible by posting on social media, sending emails to your list or simply telling people about it. Of course, you can still tease your audience ahead of the go live, but the real effort happens once the product or service is out there and ready to sell.

Alternatively, you can build up excitement and antici-pation before launching your product or service on a specific date with a big bang. In this case you want to consider when and how you're dropping hints and how to build the interest with a competition, challenge, master-classes or a give-away. Depending on the strategy that you decide to go with, you can then think through what collat-eral you need to have in place and how much of it you want to prepare ahead of time. This could be social media posts, emails, lining up influencers that could share your product, slide decks for masterclasses, outlines for chal-lenges, possibly PR or even schedule and organise in-person events where possible and feasible. Make sure you have a mix of at least two or three different ideas you can prepare and want to implement to tell your audience all about your great product or service. You want to make sure you're unmissable when you're ready to share your gift with the world!

Next, think through your customer journey, based on the work you've done so far. You want to ensure there aren't any duplicate emails or gaps in the process that could lead to confusion or manual intervention as you add all these new steps for the launch to the sales process. You also want to make sure you deliver a premium experience or at least one that is in line with the price of your product or service as well as your brand identity. For example, if you order a desk from eBay, you're relatively happy as long as it arrives undamaged and in a decent amount of time. If, however, you spend $850 on a desk from a premium furniture supplier, then you'd expect order updates, a tracking number from the logistics provider and possibly even someone that assembles it in your room of choice, right? Map out the journey and think through how you want to interact with the client (personally, system, etc.), what you need to put in place for this to happen (template emails, calendar system, email form, purchase confirmation, etc.) and who could own each step of the journey (even if it's all with you right now, it wouldn't have to be in the future).

You should have a very clear plan of what's needed now so you can start creating the assets. This would be all the emails, social media posts, slide decks for the master-class or webinar. All the things you listed above. Once you have created them, you want to schedule as much of the content as you can so that you can focus on showing up, being visible, responding to questions and just generally connecting with your audience during the actual launch. Once all of this is in place, you're ready to go live.

Go Live

This is the big one - the day you've been waiting for and working towards. I'm not going into too much detail, because it's pretty much clear what's needed from you now: you want to sell and deliver what you promised (and even that little bit extra to surprise and delight your customers). This is when you can turn them into life-long supporters and fans. Be there for them, support them, answer their questions. Even if they aren't buying from you right now, they are paying attention.

Putting it all together

I famously (using the term 'famous' very loosely here) go on about how much I hate writing a plan, even though I spent most of my career as a programme manager and writing project plans *should* be my sweet spot. Guess what - it really, *really* isn't. Not because I can't do it, but because I hate it. I hate it because it's usually out of date more quickly than I can write it so I don't see the point (I hate waste - of time and effort or ideas).

That doesn't mean I never plan anything or advise my clients to 'just go with the flow', because that's not right either. However, what I propose instead is to create a roadmap with key milestones or deliverables and then only plan the next step in more detail. How many times have you put blood, sweat and tears into long-term plans, only to feel a failure if you don't reach the finishing line? My answer is simple: plan short term for long term success, because I've got a theory; planning long-term stops us from achieving greatness.

If you've just spat your coffee out in shock, bear with me. There's a method to my madness, I promise. I believe that long-term goals set you up for failure. And it isn't *you* that is failing your goals. Your goals are actually failing you. Our lives and circumstances are constantly changing. These rapid changes ultimately impact how much we can achieve and deliver. A rigid long term plan ignores those twists and turns in the road. It doesn't account for the bumps along the way. And it can feel pretty terrifying. You may have a long-term goal of buying a house. Perhaps it's to finally go on that adventure holiday you've always dreamed of. Please don't get me wrong; those goals?

They're fantastic. I'm here for them - I'll be your cheer-leader over in the corner. But, the best way to make those goals a reality rather than just a dream is to think small and plan short.

Short-term goals are the stepping stones to your ulti-mate vision. They're the means of bringing those glittering ideas to fruition. As a general rule, we tend to know what the next week or two looks like. We'll have a rough idea of our commitments and schedule, meaning we can realisti-cally and easily factor in short-term actions that will enable us to move closer to our aspirational destination. This means that we can adjust plans - such as the quantity of work on our desk or the number of appointments in our diary - the moment we realise we have overcommitted. It's a quick issue to solve, rather than building a mountain out of a molehill. Hence, we minimise the stress attached to our goal planning: gold star number one. It's also far simpler to focus on what is right in front of us. Endless "to-do" lists that only ever seem to grow are an immediate motivation killer, and the never ending collection of things you *still need to do* is only going to destroy your buzz. Step by step, little by little, is a more productive way to tackle the journey.

Plus, it practices consistency - the ultimate saviour of productivity. It may feel counterintuitive at first, but small, incremental steps lead to the big, bad-ass results. It's achievable; practical. Setting yourself the task of "working on it all weekend" or "spending 24 hours straight with the laptop" probably isn't going to happen. No, not because you aren't determined (because I KNOW you are), but because life loves to throw us a curveball. However, one of the top reasons I'm a short-term goal kind of woman is that it allows for iterative development. When you're stuck in stone with months worth of planning, a spanner in the works (albeit, a brilliant spanner) can really mess things up. When you learn something new about your client, or spot something a competitor is doing, or have a dazzling light-bulb moment, it isn't straight forward to react and adjust. Yet, if you're working to short-term goals, you can efficiently slot those movements into the plan and come out with something even better.

Defining milestones

Just a quick note here before we go any further as I can only imagine how much resistance you're feeling right now and that you're wondering whether it'd actually accelerate this whole thing if you skipped to the next bit. I know this isn't sexy or exciting stuff which is why hardly any coach ever talks about it. Planning and systemising are almost taken for granted and, to some of you it will be common sense. BUT at the same time, I know that it's always significantly more difficult to do for yourself and your own business even if you're usually a planning-ninja. No, you're not a fraud - everything is always more difficult when we have to apply it to ourselves. Back to defining your milestones though.

There are two ways to approach this: (1) you estimate how long each of the tasks takes and base your target date based on this estimate, or, (2) set a date by when you want to launch and then plan backwards.

Start by defining your deliverables based on the list you created above, such as

- create lead magnet
- set up funnel;
- confirm product feasibility;
- etc.

Now put them in a logical order. For example, you want to design your lead magnet first, then write and set up your email sequence before you create your funnel and so on. This is great to do with sticky notes on a blank wall where you can move them around, but you can also make an excel spreadsheet work. Add dates to each of the deliverables next and work them out depending on the best approach (estimate of effort required versus backward planning). This is the foundation of your plan and these dates will also drive your more detailed, short-term plan of actions to be completed.

Planning out actions

When I spoke about short-term plans above, I don't mean that it absolutely has to be two weeks or a month. You can decide how far ahead you're comfortable planning and you may also flex this a little, depending on the work needed for a specific deliverable, i.e. you don't want to just create a plan for half a deliverable because that's as much as you can get done in a fortnight. You want to find a balance of it not becoming an all day planning exercise (that you never have time for) and not having a clue of what to do next. What you absolutely want to avoid is that you find yourself with spare time, but you don't know what to work on next. So not having a plan and tasks broken down and prioritised will always slow you down. You'll spend 30 minutes looking through to-do lists and emails and doing some low-value activities such as responding to Facebook messages, when you could have spent it brainstorming that new retreat you want to offer.

By the way, another hurdle is if you know what you want to work on, but can't find the research or documents you need to complete the task. If your (virtual) office is all over the place and you have notes in apps, notebooks, diaries, Google docs, some documents in your filing cabinet, in-tray and scanned in the cloud, then good luck. And I'm not telling you to only ever take notes in one place, because I love a notebook but also use notes apps.

However, I will tell you to take 15-30 minutes at the end of each week to organise your notes:

- capture actions in a task management system;
- add notes and ideas to the relevant resource bank; and
- schedule anything that's urgent or has a deadline.

This also shows that mapping out actions or at least re-prioritising them can be part of your weekly planning exercise or your weekly wrap up, as long as you make sure that it becomes part of a routine that you trust. It doesn't have to be a huge exercise and it doesn't have to be perfect.

To plan out the individual actions that it'll take to deliver the desired outcome, you want to list out everything it would take to make it happen. Let's use the example of 'create lead magnet' that I used above, and break this down into actions:

Decide on format;

Outline content;

Write copy;

Design asset (workbook, checklist, quiz);

Save on drive and change setting to allow people with links to access.

It may take you extra steps, such as researching lead

magnet ideas, finding a graphic designer, briefing a copy-writer, etc. This very much depends on what the lead magnet you're creating looks like, how much you can do yourself, and how much you feel you can get done in one go. You could, for example, break 'write copy' down further to "write bio", "write introduction", "write instructions", "write checklist", and so on.

If you're still in a full-time role, then I would aim to set myself the goal of completing three of these actions per week. It may not feel like much and some weeks you may get this done and find yourself with some spare time, but if you're organised and always have the next deliverable broken down into tasks, then you'll be able to jump onto the next thing. You'll also find that some weeks you only get one or two of your three goals completed and that's ok. We have to accept this and keep going.

Accountability is the difference between success and failure

I know it's not the first time that I've mentioned this, but it's so important when speaking about setting goals, creating plans and implementing them: You do not have to do this on your own! I'd actually go further than that and say that it's almost impossible to do on your own because of the time it takes and the many highs and lows that come with it. But it's also a fact that we get more done when we have to answer to someone else. Earlier on in the book I referred to the deadlines in our corporate roles, or how we often deliver things we have promised others while putting off the work that matters to us. It's ridiculous how we don't like to let other people down but don't even blink as we're not sticking to commitments we make to ourselves. Of course, there are different types of people and it's difficult to list specific characteristics. Based on my experience, the speed of delivery is task-related and whether something is in our zone of genius or not. I'm a very structured person. I like to have a plan and know what the next steps are. I also like to be prepared and don't want to be caught not having the answer, BUT I still work so much better under pressure. Sometimes this is because it's a task I dread and therefore - stupidly - put it off for as long as I possibly can. This usually relates to things my accountant needs… But it's also the stuff that is way out of my comfort zone, such as writing this book.

I committed to this last year… and then hardly did anything for months and months. I had a baby too, to be fair, but I didn't do much writing. Eventually, my lovely Business Manager Sandra asked me about progress during our quarterly strategy call, when I was planning to wrap it up by. I'm not a hundred percent sure now, but I'd bet I was scrunching up my face at that point while awkwardly fidgeting in my chair. I knew for a fact that I'd really feel the pressure the minute I put a date to it and then I'd have to deliver. And that's EXACTLY what happened. We agreed a date, I confirmed the timeline with the publisher, calculated my final draft date based on that and then figured out the number of words I'd have to write each day to deliver on time. Further to that I promised Sandra that I'd send her a picture of my daily word count on Slack every single day. And then she said to me "Don't break that chain!" Damn. But guess what - it works. I have not had a single day of not hitting my target, but instead I'm usually exceeding it because it means I get it done sooner. And yes, I am very competitive. You're now holding this book in your hand, so you know I did it. But you also know I couldn't have done it on my own.

This problem with our comfort zone is a big one when it comes to building a business, because it'll be your default state for a while. Especially during that initial period while you're wearing all the hats, you'll have to do things you won't know how to do and you'll have to do things that you really don't like doing. You'd better get used to dealing with this and take action anyway, and I've shared some tips in the box below to help you get into the habit.

As a minimum, you need to explicitly commit to your goal and tell someone else about it. The more people know, the less likely you're going to give up and not follow through - because you'd be embarrassed. But you also want to make sure that you have someone that is not your friend or family member, who keeps you on track. I've already told you why, but also remember that not everyone understands the 'short-term pain, long-term gain' sentiment that we often know too well as entrepreneurs.

Apart from setting goals, sharing these with someone else and having regular check-ins on progress, you also want to go back to the work on excuses that you did right at the beginning of the book. You know your weaknesses and most common excuses, so be honest with yourself and come up with a strategy of how you're going to overcome each of them. Try and take the emotion out of this.

Whether it's a formal business or life coach, or a fellow business owner, have a "go-to" selection of people that can cheer you on when times get tough. Picture them as your little dose of motivation when you're running on empty. You can keep them in the loop about your deadlines and expectations; they can then check in on you and give you a much-needed nudge when you veer off track. Plus, they can celebrate your successes with you! I know exactly who to call if I'm having 'one of those days' and those people know exactly when to tell me to take a break for a couple of days and then have a look at things with a fresh pair of eyes (because sometimes we need that permission), or when to keep going to get something specific done to then feel better afterwards (because sometimes taking action is the cure).

Tips on how to break out of your comfort zone

First up - you want to move into your stretch zone, but stay out of the panic zone. Which is totally possible. There are just a few simple things you need to keep in mind. I've drawn together my five tips for leaving your comfort zone and stepping into genuine success. Make yourself comfortable and get ready to dive headfirst into the *magical place*.

Breakout of your comfort zone tip #1 - Pick your battles.

Let's face it - leaving your comfort zone is going to require a huge deal of effort and energy. You need to make sure that it's worth it. Before you throw yourself in, consider whether this move is in line with your dreams and vision. Will it take you closer to them? Is it a part of the bigger picture?

If the answer is no, then perhaps it isn't worth the pressure.

Breakout of your comfort zone tip #2 - Understand the fear.

First of all, it's important to accept that you WILL have the fear: it's inevitable, nine times out of ten. But understand what kind of fear it should be. There are so many different types of fear. While some keep us totally rooted to the spot (anyone ever tried a bungee jump?), others will drive us forward. It's a spark, firing up your stomach and lighting up your adrenaline. This fear should feel like that time you had to perform in the school play (nervous but excited… butterflies galore, kind of vibes) rather than when you lost your kid in the supermarket (cue immediate stress, panic and over-whelm). If you're venturing into that second form of fear, it might be worth pressing the brakes; even just for the time being. Remember; you want to avoid the panic zone at all costs. Your health and wellbeing have to come first.

Breakout of your comfort zone tip #3 - Adapt your perception.

When you're trying to do something different (and maybe even a tad alien), it's great to picture yourself as the person that is doing it already. Why? Visualisation! Doing this will alter your inner narrative and allow you to embrace more confidence and self-belief. You want to write a book? Call yourself a writer. You want to start a business? Call yourself an entrepreneur. You want to be known for your amazing TED talk? Call yourself a speaker. I'm not asking you to update your LinkedIn head-line and redesign your business cards, but even just this subtle switch in self-talk can work wonders when it comes to plucking up the courage to take the leap.

Breakout of your comfort zone tip #4 - Embrace the new normal.

Fear of the unknown is often worse than the reality itself. The anticipation can leave your head running round and round in circles, struggling to jump off of the hamster wheel of anxiety. So, instead, try to embrace the new normal. Perhaps it's welcoming a new baby… or heading to University… or dealing with a global pandemic. Whatever the new normal is, there are countless times in life when we are pushed out of our comfort zone without even realising it. Sure, we're nervous; maybe even terrified. But we deal with it. We adapt. We learn and we grow. Essentially, when we are forced into a new way of living, we don't have the time to question it. Try to keep hold of this mentality when approaching the stretch zone.

Breakout of your comfort zone tip #5 - Take it one step at a time.

I know, I know; this is your happy place, isn't it? Your comfort zone has become cosy. It's safe, and has been for years. Expecting yourself to bounce right out of it would be bonkers. Instead, take smaller steps. Bit by bit; slowly does it. Those steps could be totally unrelated to your ultimate goal. Just something - anything! - new in your day to day life. We do this to make 'trying something new' a habit. It becomes a muscle, one we gradually stretch until the moment we're ready to pelt over the starting line of that metaphorical marathon. It doesn't have to be a major change. Maybe you've been having the same Rigatoni al forno at your local Italian for years (with zero disappointments, naturally), and one month try a different restaurant for a change. Or you try a new route to work. Could you sleep on the other side of the bed? Or buy a different brand of wine? Would you be open to trying a new hobby that you've always flirted with but never quite committed? Take a look at the areas in your life that are heading towards autopilot and mix them up. Once you start working your mind and actions in this alternative way, leaving your comfort zone won't feel so scary after all. Ultimately, the key is to stop seeing your 'safe place' as a good place to be. Instead, set yourself up for success by making sure you're prepared for whatever your stretch zone will bring, are aligned to your goals, and know exactly why you're taking this leap in the first place.

YOUR POWER SUPPORT SYSTEM

"There are no secrets to success. It is the result of preparation, hard work and learning from failure."

I'll be honest with you: this chapter isn't the most exciting one in the book, BUT it could potentially be the most important. The admin part of business is boring, but without it there is no business. I'm adding this in here, because most coaches and consultants don't, when having your back office set up will make the difference between 'making a little extra' and 'strategically working towards replacing and exceeding the income from your 9 - 5' and therefore giving you options!

You're finally at a stage where you have launched your business and are hopefully working with your first clients. You're probably realising that it's still difficult to juggle your day job and your clients at times, but you make it work. It's exciting and also rewarding and the first step on the path to freedom!

But, day job or not, the running of a business is incredibly time-consuming. The obvious tasks such as managing another inbox, arranging appointments, preparing calls with clients and following up afterwards, all take time. However, you'll soon find that there are other tasks, such as content production, which are even more relentless. If you're building an online business or even a service based business (online or not), your online presence and the messages you're sharing are your shop window. Also, it's unlikely you'll want to stick to just one service, so you'll have to go through some of the work I've outlined in this book to develop the new offering. But this is the stuff that you'll love and are excited about: exploring new ideas, having conversations with your clients or prospects to understand how you can make things even better for them, developing your unique proposition and message. Which makes it even more important to set your back office up to take as little time as possible. Getting clear on what needs to be done, your company's way of doing it and which resources you need to deliver this is key. Processes will make your performance more reliable, can include checkpoints for known points-of-failure, save you time and headspace and enable you to delegate, delegate, delegate. The goal is to free up time for you to do more of the things that you went into business for in the first place and, of course, enable you to start, run and scale your business on a part-time basis.

Introducing Systems

Let's talk about systems. I know you're probably fidgeting in your seat with excitement and anticipation… not. But I'm German, so humour me. Thinking in systems is just another way to create 'buckets' of work that you need to get done to keep your business running. Grouping similar stuff together to leverage synergies (starting to sound more exciting already, huh?). Not only that, but it's easier to identify pieces of work that you can package up and outsource when you're ready. Also, you want to make sure you can become more efficient by not just seeing individual tasks and processes, but how they fit together. For example, you don't just want to have a process for creating blog posts, but you want to make sure that you turn the blog posts into a number of social media posts before doing a Facebook live on the topic. Repurposing is for winners!

When setting up your back office, you need to balance the demands of your business: Business-as-usual, which is your client work, social media management and expenses, etc. as well as your projects, which are one-offs or less regular such as creating a new product or service, or planning your annual strategy. Taking care of both is important. Some of the business-as-usual systems you'd want to establish in your business are the operational system, content creation system, a sales system and a financial system and then a project system, which I always recommend as this is a huge growth driver.

Your operational system is the centre and umbrella of your business. It's about the things you need on a daily basis, such as your cloud-based filing system, choosing and implementing your core applications such as an email marketing system, a task management system or an app to take and organise notes, etc. The processes in your operations system could have to do with business travel, customer service, delivering your service, management of supplier relationships or process improvement. Eventually, this may also cover roles and job descriptions, but I wouldn't worry about this yet. I mentioned before how important it is to have a clear list of actions and upcoming tasks, so that you can react quickly when you find yourself with spare time. It's equally important to have an organised office so that when you have time, you know exactly what you need to work on and can find the outline of that blog post that you jotted down on the train the other day without having to search for half an hour. I mentioned this right at the start when we were looking at ways to save time: not being organised is such a drain on your resources!

As mentioned above, content is key in business, so your content creation system is super important. Content shows up everywhere: in your email sequences, your sales pages, social media posts, newsletter or your blogs, vlogs and podcasts - depending on what you choose to use in your business. The challenge with content is to deliver quality consistently. It's not difficult to put something out there every day, but it could be damaging if the quality is poor. Equally, if you put really high-quality content out but only once in a blue moon, so your audience always has to remind themselves who you are and why you're in their inbox, then that doesn't help you get them to know, like and trust you either. The key to making this work is (some) preparation. 'Some' because you can absolutely have some spontaneous content going out, responding to news or having some fun with your audience (e.g. 'One business lesson you've learned from the Tiger King? GO!"). To set this up, you want to get really clear where in your business and processes you need content, brainstorm topics that you want to cover off (such as themes for months, then topics for each week) and then organise your schedule to make sure you have time to produce it. To give you an example, I write and schedule all of my social media posts on a Monday for the week ahead. I know people that block out a whole day to write and schedule content for the month or a weekend for a quarter, but for me this feels overwhelming (and like a lot of pressure - imagine I have an off-day that day!). You have to find your personal sweet spot. Think about possible templates that would help you structure your thoughts, such as a blog outline, the content calendar mentioned above or a social media plan and create those. Lastly, create the content and repurpose! Don't think *everything* has to be original, but instead you can turn your blog post, podcast or YouTube Video into a newsletter topic, Instagram captions, content for a Face-book Live, a webinar or Facebook post or even an audio file (that your audience can conveniently listen to while walking their dog).

Your sales system definitely overlaps with operations and content, so you'll have a lot of this covered already. However, you want to map out your end-to-end customer journey (if you haven't already done so) to make sure you're not missing anything and it's a smooth process for your clients, but also needs as little interaction from you as possible - unless you consciously choose to add a personal touch. Review what you need to have in place for each step of the process, what the interaction with the customer is and what you want this to look like (personal touch versus automatic), and who could own this step of the process (if it's not you). Think in roles, not people - for example, a Virtual Assistant or a Customer Service Manager. Mapping out the customer journey will also give you a clear idea and list of possible resources you need and content you'll need to create, which in turn will feed into your other systems again.

Your financial system is likely the first piece of work you'll outsource. Getting an accountant was top of the list for me even before I started my business. In fact, I hired my accountant first and then paid her to register my company so I wouldn't make any mistakes. A lot of us (me included) get nervous when it comes to money and taxes. No one wants to get on the wrong side of the tax man, do they? Therefore, having your financial system in order is important and can remove a huge headache for you. Remember, no finances and taxes means no business, so embrace it. You want to have a clear plan of how to take care of invoicing, accounts and your expenses. Make sure you schedule in the time to deal with these because they'll otherwise become your favourite items to move down the to do list when life gets too busy.

Lastly, you want to set up a project system to deliver growth initiatives reliably and consistently. Take it from a Project Manager, anything new you tackle in life or business could be seen as a project, as long as it's a defined piece of work, has to be delivered in a set timeframe and - especially for those side hustling - has to be delivered in addition to EVERYTHING ELSE. Having this system in place means you avoid the feeling of overwhelm when first starting to work on something new. I, for one, always want to dive right in when I have an idea. I often thought I could work nights and every weekend to make this happen because I'm full of excitement. That usually lasts about a couple of days and I'm back in my ideally-hitting-the-sheets-at-9-pm-routine. I know I'm not the only one that does this and I also know that this is the reason why so many ideas never become reality: at the point where we feel overwhelmed, we often just step away from it, thinking it's not the right time and we'll look at it again soon. That soon never comes and before we know it, we find out through very irritating Facebook Ads that someone else is launching OUR IDEA.

I don't want that to happen for you just because life is too busy, because it always is - remember? But we don't make excuses anymore, so that's that. Having a clear structure (I see another checklist in the making...) to break the idea down into actionable steps is key here, which we've already covered loads in this book in different forms, but I'll include it here again to make it easier for you.

Your 'Business Case' aka your why: The business case is your justification for the project on the basis of its expected benefit, so your reason for going after this goal. It's important to have a clear idea of what the outcome will look like and feel like, and what this will mean for you personally. Also, to close the loop, you want to make sure it is in line with your business model whenever you create something new.

The What: What are the outcomes that you need to achieve to make your project a success and ensure you deliver your 'business case' (= making sure it's worth your time).

The Plan: Set some dates, but only for the key milestones and then go into more detail for the next step only - just like you did when you planned the implementation of your launch offer. I wouldn't want you to waste your time on long-term planning, but sometimes there are certain dates that are relevant (because you have to apply for funding by a certain date, because it's Christmas and you need to get your new offer out in time for that, or because you need to give notice on your job or shop premises when the lease is up) and can provide some structure, so map those out to help you decide what to tackle first.

The Resources: When planning a project, you want to make sure you have a clear view of what resources you need to make it happen. Consider time, money and people that can help. Just like in a corporate context, you'll need to free up those resources by giving up something else (=reallocation of workload). Maybe your husband can't help you build your website, but he may be able to cook three nights a week so that you have an extra hour to spend on content creation. Don't be scared to ask people for help.

The Risks: As with any major undertaking, there will be challenges to overcome and bullets to dodge. It's not meant to be easy, or everyone would do it - always remember that. The good news is that you can manage anything practical, but the biggest risks to your dream not coming true is your mindset. Name and shame your excuses and find ways to avoid them or deal with them when they do come up for you. Just like you would create a contingency plan for your business, you want to create one for your project too. Bonus: This should be so much easier now that you've done much of the work we discussed at the beginning of the book!

Progress: You're pretty much ready to get to work on this, but there is some admin I want you to do now to set yourself up for success and to ensure someone is holding you accountable. While planning this, and especially the action you are going to take in this first week, try and be as realistic as possible. I know you are raring to go, but life still happens and you have clients to see and work to do, so start by planning in 30 minutes a day. If you get more done, then that's brilliant and will motivate you, but I don't want you to feel disappointed when you didn't manage to get it all done. It's little things such as time blocking the 30 minutes in your diary for the first week and also putting in some time to review progress and focus for the next week. If you can get into a routine around this, then life will be so much easier.

Spending a little time before you get to work will pay off in the long run and will help you stay consistently even if the initial excitement wears off.

Documenting your Operations

Once you know which system you need in your business and what those systems include, you can document the processes (or activities) involved. When you think of processes, you're likely thinking of A0 sheets of paper with thousands of little boxes, each representing a task or a decision. Business Process Management is a big deal in the corporate world and it may send a shiver down your spine when you remember how process reviews were usually followed by redundancies. Never nice, whether you're impacted yourself or not. And those massive process maps were the last thing you needed to be able to do your job. I mean, who pulls out a map that covers three desks to double-check whether to do A or B first. Most of us would rather do it wrong!

So, I get that processes aren't the first thing you think of when you start your own business, BUT it's something that you HAVE TO think about as soon as you're ready to grow and scale. They'll be the foundation of your business as they bring some of the below benefits.

Standardising your processes will save you energy when completing the task because thinking about what needs doing and how to do it won't take up headspace. You won't have to worry about forgetting anything (such as checking for SEO when posting a blog post) so can execute repetitive tasks that don't require your creative input more quickly, leaving more time and energy for those tasks that inspire you and really move the needle.

Defining how things are done will make sure that your customers are experiencing the same level of service independent of who is looking after them as you grow. You want your processes to be simple, logical and repeatable to make them easy to get right and really, really hard to get wrong. I've mentioned automation before and this is the first step towards this as you think through the most straightforward way to do something, which will ultimately also make it easier to automate.

Documenting your processes, including the likely points of failure and their mitigating actions, as well as guidance on what to do in exceptional cases, significantly reduces the risk in your business. It enables others to be fully aware of what can happen and to troubleshoot when things don't go to plan, giving you more peace of mind. Something as simple as a checklist (which is really nothing more than the to do list we write ourselves each day) can make a huge difference to someone - even if they are experts at something and do it day in and day out. It's like going shopping and being unsure of whether you turned the hob off at home. It's these mundane everyday tasks that we sometimes forget because we're not thinking about it in detail, but are just going through the motions.

Lastly, as part of documenting your processes, you create the resources and put the systems in place that support the delivery of those processes. These will save you time, support you (and your team) in delivering the best service possible for your clients and deliver back-office (=non-revenue-generating) tasks as efficiently as possible. If we don't do this work, we often get caught in a never-ending cycle of reinventing the wheel, recreating resources and tools that we need to use over and over. This could be proposal templates, intake questionnaires for new clients or social media content calendars, for example.

As you can see from this list, documenting your processes doesn't only add value if you have a team or are planning to outsource work, but can also make your life easier and save you lots of time and energy. If you don't start thinking about this from the start, then you'll get to a point at which you're too busy to do all the work and can't scale any further, but also don't have time to document processes before finding and onboarding a team. Therefore, I always recommend to capture this information as you progress, bearing in mind that it doesn't have to be polished (because I don't want you to use this as an excuse not to launch!) but can be a simple list of bullet points that outlines steps you take to do something. Polishing, branding and structuring it could be something for your first team member to complete as they're going through the onboarding process.

Types of process documents

There are three ways of how to document processes, which I want to cover really quickly to make sure you consider what's the best fit for you and for the process or procedure you want to document.

Step-by-Step: This format is great when we need a step-by-step process to happen, with a specific order. They typically are READ-DO, which means: 1) you READ the instructions; 2) you DO the task. Step-by-step process descriptions are great for the training of new employees or employees that are taking on a new task. Recipes are an example of this type of process.

Checklist: Checklists are helpful when there are a number of tasks that need to be completed to produce an output, but the sequence isn't relevant. However, we now often find numbered checklists in procedures which do ask for a specific sequence. They are DO-CONFIRM, which means: 1) you DO the tasks, usually from memory, once you're good at it; 2) you CONFIRM completion of the task.

Guidelines: Guidelines to act and make decisions by

do not follow a chronological order or are broken down step-by-step. They are best for situations with a lot of exceptions and variables, such as dealing with complaints. Guidelines can suggest a certain style while incorporating some things to remember; e.g. "When dealing with complaints, always maintain a warm energy and listen to the customer. Establish all the facts and avoid getting confrontational, no matter how rude the customer becomes."

For your business, especially at an earlier stage, checklists and guidelines should be fine, especially if you're creating resources and templates too and want to mostly provide guidance on how to complete them.

Writing a checklist

Start by brainstorming a list of steps. Write down everything you can think of to deliver the specific process or task you're creating a checklist for, before thinking through the most common reasons that things go wrong and build in mitigating actions. Turn the list into actionable steps

Create DO steps and put these in chronological order where possible, but bear in mind that some steps can happen in parallel. That's ok and you can point that out on the checklist. Also include check-ins or sign off from key stakeholders (such as yourself, if you're writing the checklist for someone else) as items on the list. Then test it by running through your checklist and actually completing it to check for completeness. Even better, get someone else to trial it and get their feedback. Finally, tweak it! This is not set in stone and the more you use it, the more you'll want to refine it. Not only because you may have missed something at the beginning, but also because you'll be optimising the process, outsourcing part of it or creating templates, etc. Things change so quickly, so make sure you do update it as and when you realise that there is a better way to do something.

Some tips for success: Bear in mind, that there will always be different audiences with different levels of experience, so use subheadings to structure the document for easy skimming for those that don't need the detail, but use it to double-check. You can also include different forms of media (pictures, screenshots, flow-diagrams or even video) in the document, especially for more complex procedures. Make sure you create a separate document for each process to avoid confusion. Ensure you have a plan in place to review and update the process documents regularly. Keep a central log of your process documents, the date of the last update and link them in the log for easy reference and store documents online (e.g. on Google Drive) for easy access.

I appreciate that documenting processes isn't going to be one of your priorities when you first start off. And it may not be absolutely necessary for a while, but you also want to start before you're ready to make sure you have the capacity to do this exercise, as I mentioned previously. I often suggest to my clients to capture one or two processes each week to build your foundation, step-by-step. Remember that you'll also hire help earlier than others because of the limited time and energy you have to spend on your business.

Building your team

Let's be honest here… People management can be hard and definitely isn't everyone's cup of tea. I know many business owners that became their own boss so they wouldn't have to manage a team, which often is a side effect of climbing the corporate ladder. Whether you feel it takes too much time and energy away from the work you really want to do, it's something you're just not good at, or both, it is often something we consider as we decide what kind of business we're looking to build and how big a business we are aiming for. Not many of us are dreaming of starting the next Google or Amazon, right?

I get that and agree, even if I personally would love to build a team and have an office with my name on the door. At the same time, I want you to understand that there are limits to how big and successful you can grow your side hustle without burning out if you're unwilling to get help. And there are ways to grow your team, without the headaches that come with people management, that are more flexible: Outsourcing rather than hiring. You still want to make sure you find the right people, of course. People that care about your business as much as their own, that deliver work of the highest standard, on time and on budget.

I often hear from my clients (and friends) how they've worked with a VA/Copywriter/Social Media Manager/etc. before, "but it didn't work out" and now they're hesitant to try again. When I ask them what jobs they gave them, how they equipped them to do those jobs and so on, they look at me blankly. Two things: First of all, you must understand that even the best Virtual Assistant in the world won't be able to read your mind. Secondly, just because they do something different to you (especially if you haven't specifically told or taught them otherwise), doesn't mean it's not right, or worse. Of course, there are things that are specific to your brand that you want to be done in a certain way, but you need to make sure that whoever completes those tasks has the knowledge and tools available to deliver them in the way you expect.

Before you go out looking for help or ask for recommendations, get really clear on what you need help with. You'll have an idea, based on the work you did in the earlier chapter on finding partners as well as your outlined systems and the processes you're capturing, but make sure you list it all out and bundle similar tasks together. Then decide whether you're looking for support on an ongoing or ad-hoc basis. For example, even if you're clear that you're looking for a copywriter, you need to decide whether you're looking for someone that you can pay on a retainer basis to write a certain number of blog posts each month, or if you want them to write a sales page and email sequence for your launch offer as a defined project. Alternatively, there may be a difference in the type of Virtual Assistant you're looking for depending on whether you want someone to manage your inbox, arrange your meetings with clients and book your travel (so 2019, I know…) or you need someone to help you build your funnel and connect your payment portal to your course platform. These are just a couple of examples of very different skill sets which could lead to very disappointing results if you're hiring first and then deciding what you'd like them to take off your plate.

So, outline tasks first, group them together and then go out and ask for recommendations. Once you've found someone you want to work with, make sure you take time to onboard them, train them, and agree on ways of working with them (again, they can't mind read). When onboarding them, create an email address for them, give them access to critical folders and information (such as logos, process documents, checklists and so on) and intro-duce them to other internal or external members of your team, if applicable. Don't worry, it's very likely that your new help has lots and lots of experience in setting up new clients, so will likely guide you through the process which means you don't have to think too much about this as long as you have tasks and your process descriptions ready.

By the way, the same principles apply to suppliers and partners as to building a team internally: You always want to find someone that's an expert in their field and knows more than you do. If you do, then you can let go, trust them to do a great job and even learn from them - which comes back to the point I made above about how some-thing is not necessarily worse, just because it wasn't done the way you do it.

A word on delegating

You have some of your procedures defined and could get the help, but - and it's probably more of a BUT - you have tried delegating before, it didn't play out well, and you now know that it is often easier to do it yourself, so you know it's done right. Thinking about it makes you cringe though, because you also know (a) you can't do it all and (b) that's not exactly what leadership is about, is it? Let's agree that delegation is an art. An art that you will soon master and this is how:

1. Prioritise

Obvious, right? Again, easier said than done. I won't tell you how to prioritise because there are too many variables: deadlines, importance, size of the task. I would suggest you map out the actions you are aware of and when they should be delivered by (we'll go into more detail on planning real soon).

You can now clearly see what needs doing, and seeing the outcomes next to each other makes it easier to identify those you can delegate compared to those you would struggle to give to someone else.

———

2. The what, the why and the how

Tell them what you want them to do, the why and how you want them to do it (if necessary). The what and why are essential: You want to be specific in defining the outcome you expect and how delivering this will benefit the larger project, or the bigger goals of your company. The 'why' is almost always forgotten, but it serves two important purposes: (a) it challenges you to think about whether the task is actually needed, and needed in the way you think it is, and (b) it acts as a motivator for the person completing the task because it will give their work meaning (ideally, we want to build long standing relationships with our suppliers, so this is relevant). Note: You should only detail the 'how' if you absolutely have to, e.g. if it is a customer requirement. If you're hiring the right people, then they should know how to do it better than you do.

––––––––

3. Name the date

I should think that this goes without saying, but yet again there are two reasons to make sure you name the date that you need them to deliver. First of all, you can make sure you have what you need when you need it - this is obvious. Secondly, it will give the person doing the work the opportunity to manage expectations about their capacity.

––––––––

4. Ensure understanding

This simple step takes 2 minutes and can save you hours and days in the process. Just let them repeat back to you what they think they are doing, how and when by. Give more input or guidance if there are questions or if they have misunderstood. Simple!

––––––––

5. Check-in

Depending on the size and duration of the task or project, either set some reminders for yourself to check in with your supplier (or team member) or schedule regular catch ups so you can discuss and review progress and provide guidance. Don't forget to do this! For your sake and theirs. It will give you more comfort as you can see that the work is getting done and don't suddenly remember at 2:57 a.m. (as I tend to do), and they can work iteratively and adapt as they go along rather than deliver something that isn't right.

The hardest part of delegating is to plan all that is there is to be done, learning to let go and to transition into the CEO role that allows your business to grow beyond you. It will get easier with time, and it will be worth it!

———

Working through and implementing the above will provide you with a really strong foundation for a business that you can scale to 6-figures and beyond. Of course, there'll always be another process to map out, a person that isn't the right fit and needs to be replaced, new offers to develop, build and launch and so on, but this is your solid structure that allows you to eventually take that leap into full-time entrepreneurship. Don't skip steps and don't rush them, but enjoy this start of something huge.

ACTION PLAN

Y ou're at the end of the third and last section of the book and by now you should know:

- how to set your business up for success;
- what steps to take to turn your business model into reality; and
- how to organise your back office and team efficiently.

Because I'm a sucker for ticking things off a list, I'm including a list of actions you should complete at the end of each section:

1. Come up with a risk management plan.

2. Plan how you can structure your week differently to make time for your side hustle.

3. Deliverables and milestones for your launch offer.

4. Plan out actions for the first deliverable and schedule them in.

5. Map out your back office set up.

6. Start documenting tasks and processes on a weekly basis.

7. Identify and hire help (as needed).

YOU'RE READY TO LAUNCH!

FINAL WORDS

I started writing this book as I sat propped up in a hospital bed on the antenatal ward of my local hospital. It was early on a Sunday and I was waiting to be induced - my worst-case birth scenario. After detailed research on various Facebook groups and forums online, I was preparing myself for a labour over four days as a minimum, so I had brought my iPad to start writing this book (and watch Friends, 'cause oxytocin) for distraction. I'm telling you this because I thought back to that moment in hospital as I was considering my final words to you, because it's such a fantastic metaphor for the journey of building a business. Because not only did I bring my iPad to the hospital that day, but also enough snacks for a week, two books, essential oils and a diffuser to go with them, a

Bluetooth speaker, battery operated tea lights, refreshing face mists, a handheld fan, several comfortable outfits for various stages of the journey, several outfits for the baby, etc. As you can tell, I tried to prepare for all eventualities. None of which happened.

We often feel as though we have to approach a business the same way: anticipate all that could happen, have a plan and the answers for everything, We read all the books, buy the courses, download 47 checklists and guides to 'making 6-figures overnight', buy notebook after notebook to trick ourselves into sitting down to finally structure our idea and make a list of to do's (because there's nothing better than a brand-new notebook, right) and before we know it, another two years have passed.

Luckily, the advantage of giving birth over starting a business is the pretty solid deadline, so we can only prepare so much and then have to go with the flow. When you build a business, you need to decide on the moment to leap yourself.

My labour didn't last 4 days. Nowhere near. My beautiful baby girl Harriet was born 23 hours and 58 minutes later and is now sleeping (semi-)peacefully upstairs as I'm writing these notes to you. I obviously didn't make much progress on this book on that day last August, nor did I manage to eat many of the snacks, wear any of the outfits or use the essential oils. I did however use the handheld fan. A LOT.

So, if you've read this book from beginning to end in one go without doing the work, then please go back and take it one step at a time. Don't overthink it, but continue to take action consistently. You can't anticipate or control what exactly is going to happen or how long it'll take, but you can control the next step you're taking. Move forward and put yourself out there.

One more thing: during my many years of side hustling, I often had moments when I felt like a fraud. I was surrounded by full-time business owners and never quite measured up. Either, I wasn't progressing as quickly as they were, I couldn't join meet-ups because I was at work, I wasn't struggling financially as much as some of them and felt guilty for it (ridiculous, really). I was on a Zoom call with one of my business besties when I broke out in tears because I wasn't as successful yet as someone else in my circle and I was ashamed of the fact that I was working a multi-six figure corporate contract while I was building my business. She just stared at me with one eyebrow raised considerably as I was blowing my nose before she told me to be proud of the fact that I could secure that contract, that I was able to deliver a full-time role while building two businesses, and to own my journey.

And this is why I wrote this book. I want to create a community of those that have big dreams, but have bills to pay. I want you to be proud of this journey you're going on. You're hardworking and resilient, determined and ambitious, which is beautiful. Is it easy? Hell no. Is it worth it? Absolutely.

I'm proud of you.

STAY IN TOUCH

You can find all the bonus resources and especially The 6-Figure Side Hustle Roadmap - The Ultimate Mapping Tool to go from Idea to Income, here:

www.thesidehustlesolution.com

If you're interested in finding out more about how we can work together to build your dream business part-time, I'd love to have a chat anytime. Find all the details to get in touch with me below:

Visit: www.frederikeharms.com

Email: hello@frederikeharms.com

Follow me on:

 instagram.com/frederikeharms

ACKNOWLEDGEMENTS

When having a baby, starting a second business and writing a book coincide with a global pandemic, it can be difficult to keep going sometimes and I know I would not have been able to do this without some important people in my life.

First of all, thank you to the beautiful Abigail Horne who made me believe that I could make my dream of writing a book come true and for giving me lots of little pep talks along the journey - during the book writing and my pregnancy. Thank you for sharing my excitement!

Thank you to my mentor Laura Belgray who reminded me that I could be a writer just by writing. I've never been interested in celebrities (apart from Eminem) but have been following inspiring entrepreneurs for years and you are one of them. It was a dream come true when I finally got to meet you at your writing retreat in Italy. I found my voice and a way to express my personality in my writing, for which I'm forever grateful.

Thank you to my mentor Marisa Corcoran, who I quoted twice in this book, and my CCS squad. I started to work with you about the same time I started writing this book and I can't thank you enough for the space you have created with the CCS programme and the legendary people you've brought together who keep cheering me on. I'm forever grateful for the way you believe in me when I can't.

A huge thank you and shout out to Sandra and Laura - my dream team - who patiently accepted my daily messages with pictures of my word count to hold me accountable and who have my back on a daily basis. Nothing is too big or too small and I would not want to run this business without you both!

Amy, even if we don't see enough of each other, I know you always have my back and 'get me'. You make me laugh and I love to talk about how we're changing the world with you. You're my inspiration.

To my friends and family - I love you.

Thank you to my beautiful baby girl Hattie for making my world a better place every single time you smile at or cuddle into me. Whatever I do in life, I do for you.

Lastly, Ben. My best friend and my soulmate. Thank you so much for being my biggest fan, for believing in me whenever I can't and to always tell me how proud of me you are. And thank you for putting Hattie to bed so many nights so I could write this book. I love you.

REFERENCES

1. Thomas, Denise Duffield, *Chillpreneur: The New Rules for Creating Success, Freedom, and Abundance on Your Terms* (Hay House 2019)
2. Godin, Seth, *The Practice: Shipping creative work* (Penguin Business 2020)
3. Byrne, Rhonda, *The Secret* (Simon & Schuster UK 2006)
4. de Berker, A., Rutledge, R., Mathys, C. *et al. Computations of uncertainty mediate acute stress responses in humans* (Nat Commun 2016)
5. Pausch, Randy. *The Last Lecture* (Two Roads 2010)